claims on our attention today. His interpretation of the imagination as the peculiar human power which could induct
man into the significant forms of Christianity is also important as an escape
from the alternatives of fundamental-
ism, religious agnosticism based on science, and mysticism. And his work has
none of the easy optimism about man
and history which characterized the
Unitarians and Liberal Protestants of
his age.

Now Bushnell's life and writings have
been rescued from neglect and his
thinking presented for the first time
clearly and without distortion. Readers
of this book will discover him as one of
the noteworthy figures of a crucial period in our religious history.

About the author . . .

BARBARA M. CROSS received her Ph.D.
from Radcliffe College in 1956 and is at
present an instructor of English at Bryn
Mawr. *Horace Bushnell* was written under a fellowship from the American
Association of University Women.

HORACE BUSHNELL:
Minister to a Changing America

HORACE BUSHNELL:

Minister to a Changing America

By Barbara M. Cross

 THE UNIVERSITY OF CHICAGO PRESS

Library of Congress Catalog Number: 58-7914

THE UNIVERSITY OF CHICAGO PRESS, CHICAGO 37
Cambridge University Press, London, N.W. 1, England
The University of Toronto Press, Toronto 5, Canada

© *1958 by The University of Chicago. Published 1958*
Composed and printed by THE UNIVERSITY OF CHICAGO
PRESS, *Chicago, Illinois, U.S.A.*

To

MY MOTHER AND FATHER

Acknowledgments

I am indebted to the American Association of University Women for a grant that made completion of the research possible. The librarians and libraries of Harvard and Yale universities, of Crozer Theological Seminary, and of Swarthmore College have given me essential and generous co-operation. My outstanding obligations, however, are to Professors Oscar Handlin and Perry Miller of Harvard. I am indebted to Professor Miller for my first interest in the subject, for an appreciation of the Puritan religious tradition, and for countless insights into American intellectual and religious life, as well for encouragement and specific criticism. My debts to Professor Handlin defy enumeration. He followed the manuscript through its laborious birth and growth with provocative questions, detailed suggestions, and constant, generous concern. I am indebted to him, too, for the lectures, seminars, and books in which he communicated his original, comprehensive approach to social and intellectual history. With his customary generosity and humor, my husband made suggestions for the final manuscript and put up with the erratic temper and household accompanying my labors. Mrs. Frances Overstreet prepared the Index, for which Bryn Mawr College provided a grant-in-aid.

BARBARA M. CROSS

Introduction

My purpose in this book has been to analyze the religious thought of Horace Bushnell and the emergence of his theology from his society and tradition. Because Bushnell had to interest and address the Protestant middle class of nineteenth-century America, the book has partly become a study of the concerns and values of this group; because Bushnell was a Congregational minister, it is also an interpretation of the adjustment of Christianity to a specific time and place. Undermined by apathy, science, republican enthusiasm, and middle-class pride, American religion in the nineteenth century faced a crisis that threatened to destroy it as a viable intellectual belief. Bushnell met this crisis so successfully that his work became a turning point in American Protestantism. I have traced here the interplay between secular pressures and religious thought; I have also tried to show how the Christian faith maintained its own challenge and imperatives during all adjustments.

The reformed faith of Luther and Calvin provides a pattern by which to define Bushnell's peculiar formulation of theology, for he inherited the modified Calvinism of New England, and throughout his life the New Testament, the work of Jonathan Edwards, and contemporary orthodoxy kept the perspectives of strict Calvinism before him. Though Calvinism by Bushnell's time was notorious for its "hard points," New England had not completely retreated from its quondam faith. The basic doctrines of orthodoxy had been challenged, but they were still a going concern. Like his fellow Americans, Bushnell could not ignore Calvinism, and he worked in the light of its pervasive critique of the human condition.

The conviction of a qualitative moral disparity between God and man informed Calvinism. Born sinful, guilty, and corrupt, man could not escape the moral obliquity at the center of his personality. His acts vitiated by a depraved will, he stood before an awful and a righteous God. The knowledge of his own irredeemable guilt was his closest approach to the truth and to salvation. To escape damnation, such a creature depended absolutely upon gratuitous divine mercy.

The Calvinist God transcended man, yet ineluctably determined his fate. The human mind could not hope to fathom His ways, and He remained always mysterious, to some extent a *deus absconditus*. But He had revealed His will in the Bible, where man could read the divine law and discover his sin. And God had given man more than knowledge; to some He had given salvation itself—a gift unmerited, irresistible, unconditional, and eternal. Christ's descent and death had won atonement for those chosen by God. That grace was bestowed upon a limited number of men seemed to Calvin the *decretum horribile*, a fact both terrible and inescapable.

Though salvation was limited to the few and though hellfire was eternal, man had no just complaint. All men deserved damnation. If one were saved, he owed God an infinite, humble gratitude; if lost, a devastating penitence. To question the will of the Creator was blasphemous pride, for God's sovereignty was absolute. The human task was to serve and glorify Him and to wait humbly for a redeeming grace.

English, Scotch-Irish, and Dutch immigrants made Calvinism the predominant religion in Colonial America. In New England, where the suffrage was often restricted to church members, where the clergy spoke decisively on public affairs, and where morals were supervised by clerically enlightened officials, Calvinist perceptions informed the common experience. The theology itself was codified by Samuel Willard in the late seventeenth century; and throughout the eighteenth century, New England divines pondered and elucidated the system of the reformed faith.

In the long line of theologians, Jonathan Edwards is the dominant figure, and his genius presided over the deliberations of the later eighteenth and early nineteenth centuries. Accepting the basic premises of Calvinism, Edwards concentrated upon defining the nature of true religious experience. He explored the character of religious affections, of the will and of virtue, and assessed the marks of conversion. The half-hidden God of Calvinism remained, but His decrees, Edwards discovered, were sweet to the believer, who selflessly assented to the totality of Being. Man was bound to will the "greatest apparent good," but once the sense of divine things seized him, he had a saving experiential knowledge of the true good.

The next generations of New England divines built upon Edwards' work. These men, who studied in the parsonages of Edwards or Edwards' pupils, who assiduously read and closely argued a small number of treatises on divinity, set out to integrate theology. They produced the "New England Theology," with its peculiar doctrines of the unimputed sinfulness of every individual, the natural ability of sinners to do right, the moral-government theory of the atonement. Since the unregenerate had the natural power to repent, New Light ministers pressed ardently for the harvest of conversions known as a revival. They taught that neither Adam's sin nor Christ's obedience was imputed to the individual, whose election hinged upon God's decree. Christ had died to save God's public honor; through His suffering and death, God enforced the penalties of the Law and revealed His hatred of sin.

While New England theologians were working out God's obligations as just governor of the world, the Colonial rebellion against an unjust sovereign was creating a nation. With the beginning of the United States, divines had to meet more dilemmas than the logic of the atonement involved. Engrossed in a perilous experiment in freedom, the American people pictured themselves more easily as republicans than as sinners. They had become accustomed to stress their capacity and their natural rights more than their obligations and impotence. The rationale of the Revolution was ill suited to Calvinism, but as Locke's theories of social contract, the common sense of Thomas Paine, and Continental deism gained a hearing among American citizens and soldiers, alien ideas came to seem self-evident.

Peace and the new government revealed the declined estate of the ministry and of religion. In Virginia, where young men debated whether Christianity had proved "beneficial or injurious to mankind," Bishop Madison and John Marshall agreed that the Episcopal church could never revive. At Princeton in 1782, only two students professed themselves Christian, and at Yale, young men addressed each other as "Rousseau" and "Voltaire." In New England, when Federalist ministers tried to enlighten congregations on politics, they met indignant resistance.[1] Self-consciously and competently enlisted in an experiment in secular government, the people felt no need for theological advice on their politics.

The early nineteenth century increased the perplexities of the few New Englanders who still longed for a Calvinist Holy Commonwealth. Throughout New England, land deterioration, the beginnings of industry, the promise of the West, and the building of canals and better roads redistributed the population and changed familiar living patterns. Mobile young men in search of a fortune filled the cities; impoverished families in the villages saw sons and daughters depart for western lands or urban occupations. The stable church of the Puritan faith, the unit of God's special grace, no longer existed. Congregations fluctuated and were composed of men and women facing straitened circumstances, sudden wealth, or an unknown order in which they had to prove themselves. Meanwhile, other sects were expanding: Baptists and Methodists increased among the lower classes, Episcopalians and Unitarians among the well-to-do. In Connecticut, despite the resistance of the Congregational clergy, the union of such dissenting sects disestablished the Congregational church in 1818.

Religion scarcely monopolized the interest or enthusiasm of the country. An exuberant nationalism pervaded the North, inspiring Clay's American Plan, Webster's oratory, Emerson's *American Scholar*. In the thirties Jacksonian democrats attacked the "money power" which curtailed the laborer's and businessman's chances for success; in the forties the states fought to fulfil their continental destiny.

Bushnell shared the aggressive nationalism of his time. He inherited its religious traditions, and knew firsthand the discomforts of its social mobility. As a minister he assumed peculiar responsibility for the time's religion and morality. His audience was mixed. In Connecticut orthodoxy was vociferous and wary, but Bushnell also addressed the larger public that supported Episcopalianism, Unitarianism, or transcendentalism. The specific pressures of his audience, his class, his vocation, and his time stand behind his theology. His story necessarily becomes a partial narrative of the fortunes of Christianity in America. But it is also the record of one man's personal struggle to find and hold Christian truth for himself and for his contemporaries.

Contents

I. Origins

Like the majority of American ministers in his time, Horace Bushnell was born on a farm. For generations the Bushnells had tilled the Connecticut soil, moving from Guilford to New Canaan, Litchfield, and New Preston but not hazarding a remoter frontier. The family history and traditions had been shaped in rural Vermont and Connecticut, and the religious unrest of eighteenth-century New England marked its annals. Bushnell's paternal grandmother, unable to accept the strict Calvinism of her local minister, had been converted to evangelical, non-doctrinal Methodism by an itinerant preacher. Yet, if religious dogma had waned in the family, the religious passion persisted, and in New Preston, Bushnell's Methodist father and Episcopalian mother joined the only available church—the Congregational.

During Bushnell's childhood his parents achieved moderate prosperity and prestige within their known society. In 1805, when Bushnell was three, his father moved to New Preston to take advantage of its superior water power. Neighboring farmers brought their raw wool to the elder Bushnell's carding machine and cloth mill; eventually he became a justice of the peace. On the farm, hired laborers worked in the fields with the father and children, while Mrs. Bushnell employed several men in a cloth-dressing shop. The family lived thriftily and unpretentiously, eating their meals with the "hired hands," dressing in homespun of their own manufacture.

For eighteen years Bushnell lived in the family's roomy farmhouse, and for most of that time he expected to spend the rest of his life on a Connecticut farm. He had the farmer's sure, hard knowledge of the seasons and the soil. He tugged rocks out of the hill, threshed rye in the autumn sun, dressed flax by hand. In spring he plowed the recalcitrant soil and knew the excitement of a gusty sky and the sudden thrust of green. Winters meant hauling logs through the thick snow and being confined in the schoolroom. Trained in the industrious self-respect of small New England entrepreneurs, Bushnell received the discipline of toil and frugality. Looking back on his youth, he was proud of its severe simplicity; "the necessities of a rough country and an intractable soil are good necessities," he announced in 1851.

There were pleasures as well: bossing or playing with his younger brothers and sisters; doughnuts, cider, apples, and hickory nuts shared around a winter fire; fishing for pickerel on Lake Waramaug; yearly trips with his father to sell produce in the great city of Hartford. An active, ingenious, boisterous boy, Bushnell took his studies casually but delighted in tests of skill, pitting himself against neighboring wrestlers and debaters. His days were strenuous but not tense; the democracy of the small town permitted a buoyant assurance. Everyone wore homespun, and in the church, worshipers sat according to age while they pursued the minister's syllogisms on free will and election. Within the farming village, Bushnell was at his ease. Only the thought of the "great folk" of city and college disquieted him, and at fourteen, content with his prospects, he rejected his mother's suggestion that he go to college.[1]

Though respectfully eager to train himself for a life like his father's, the boy does not seem to have been close to his

parent. Bushnell's recorded memories of his father are dutiful but brief. Later in life, he recalled his father's Sunday
grumblings at their minister's Calvinism; eventually, he
blamed his beloved mother's death upon his father's decision
to move west late in life. He never forgot a flogging his
father gave him. In the later imaginative stabilization of his
family life, he identified this whipping with the rigor of the
Law.[2]

Bushnell was more warmly devoted to his mother, whose
love, resolution, and energy loom large in the scanty records
of his childhood. She had dedicated him, her first-born, to
the ministry, and while he was still in grade school, she persuaded her husband to give the boy a college education. Her
practical, insistent, and untheological faith eased Bushnell's
childhood religious experiences; he never suffered before a
merciless Calvinist deity the youthful terror that drove
contemporaries like Horace Mann to self-torment and theological rebellion. Though anxious to have her children
Christians, Mrs. Bushnell inquired little about their beliefs
or conversion experiences but stressed rather "industry,
order, time, fidelity, reverence, neatness, truth, intelligence,
prayer."[3]

Bushnell's love for his mother was sustained and compelling. His later concept of the Christian life incorporated
her values, and his most crucial decisions tended to fulfil her
ambitions for him. Under the impetus of her religious concern, urged by the Calvinism of the local minister, he struggled with orthodox doctrines and finally, at the age of
twenty, joined the New Preston church.

As the boy matured into manhood, his mother took increasing charge of his destiny. Between 1815 and 1820 the
expansion of manufacturing cut into the market for homespun woolens, and Bushnell's apprenticeship to his father
no longer seemed prudent. Instead of following his father's

career, he had now to make his own way. His lack of capital, his newly won faith, his mother's hopes—pointed to college and the ministry, and Mrs. Bushnell planned and carried out the household frugality that made the money available. In 1823 Bushnell left home to enter Yale's freshman class. The young man departed from New Preston as a prospective minister, spurred by his mother's sacrifices and blessed by her gratified ambition.

He arrived at Yale in the fall, older than most students and dressed in the outmoded homespun which, for economy, he had agreed to wear throughout his college career. This was his first close contact with the outside world, and it was accompanied by strain and uncertainty. By contemporary standards he was already counted a man. He came from the country, fearful of the gap between his "awkward" rural ways and the "great folk of a college." During his four years at New Haven he was ignored by the society of the city, though his classmate Nathaniel Parker Willis was so besieged with invitations that he could not find time to study. Willis, who was busily playing the gentleman, found few Yale colleagues with whom he cared to associate. Most of them were "profane and dissipated." The "pious students" were "mostly *men*, without any refinement either of manners or feeling—fresh from the country—whose piety" made them respectable and saved them from being total "boors."[4]

College life seemed to imperil piety. While Willis amused himself in Hartford society, his own religious faith declined. Parents were familiar with the subversive effects of college. "I am indeed encircled by gay companions and numerous temptations," Jonathan Brace, Jr., admitted, describing Yale in 1827 to his anxious parents. Already a sturdy, brusque, and forthright man, Bushnell roomed next to the elegant young Willis and decided that he himself cut a "poor figure." When he eventually improved his status in the college, he discovered that his "religious character" had gone "down." Yet, although Bushnell lost his faith during college, he did not overtly worry about religious problems or search out a possible rationale of belief. His college papers did not touch upon religious subjects. As a Junior he wrote a tragedy; his light essays dealt with "Jack Phosphorous," "Home," and "Dancing," while his more serious efforts investigated "Ambition" and "Genius." He devoted his commencement address to "Some Defects of Modern Oratory."[5]

The skimpy records of Bushnell's college years bear marks of diffidence and conflict. He worked hard, played boisterously at sports, joined a temperance group and a debating society; but on the whole he gave the impression of a "scholar, original, retired, peculiar." Though his letters reveal that Demosthenes had captured his imagination, he recited shyly and reluctantly. Nonetheless, the student was already convinced that man wished as inevitably for an "imperishable name as for an eternal existence."[6]

Out of the tension between his past and the demands of college society came Bushnell's first experience of language as a problem and a barrier. "I was brought up in a country family, ignorant of any but country society, where cultivated language in conversation was unknown. I entered college late, . . . when the vernacular type of language is cast. . . . I had no language, and if I chanced to have an idea, nothing came to give it expression."[7]

During these years of conscious exile he struggled to forge a language. He took the "pedestrian" Paley for a model, and his faith continued to disintegrate; he read Coleridge's *Aids to Reflection* and found it baffling. The isolation of the move from New Preston to New Haven started Bushnell on the long quest for a new understanding of language; twenty-five years later he would construct a semantic that could resolve the tensions between a rural vocabulary, sophisticated society, and Christian faith.

The uneasiness Bushnell experienced in Yale reflected the strains of the changing, mobile society of nineteenth-century America. In the Northeast, an emergent urban society was introducing standards of refinement which both beguiled and frightened men born to a simpler order. Traveling through New England and New York in 1821, Theodore Dwight recorded the rise of a new "fashionable" society; gloomily he observed the mincing, curtseying, French-speaking children paraded by proud and corrupted parents while he pondered New England's moral decay. "You would suppose," he morosely noted, "that the children were a superior race of beings." His own convictions on innate depravity unshaken, Dwight deplored the rise of an educational system which favored "an imagination, already soft, and sickly; . . . a sensibility already excessive."[8]

Fears like Dwight's troubled the *Connecticut Evangelical Magazine* and the *Christian Spectator*. Such magazines urged a new asceticism to distinguish saints from sinners—total abstinence from balls, cards, and luxury. Yet, despite pious exhortations, the giddiness of the "better classes" was not stayed, and imprecations continued to darken sermons, while a procession of reform societies publicized a backsliding public.

The simple fact was that city people were not exclusively anxious for sainthood but timidly aspired to cut an impressive figure in urban society. In a fluctuating economy the newly rich were hastily defining their estate by all the available symbols of aristocracy and were not to be checked by clerical laments. Etiquette books multiplied as the middle class determinedly marched after gentility. It was difficult to claim sure success when a steady stream of articulate travelers harped on the crudeness of Americans. Too ambitious and too diffident to dismiss foreign opinion, indignant Americans insatiably perused accounts of national vulgarity.

While privately doubting their social adequacy, Americans also worried that virtue and religion might be lost in the scramble after fashion. The mixed aims of the society found readiest expression in popular fiction, where inadmissible conflicts could be dramatically exorcised by author and reader. The gift books that ornamented American parlor tables during the early nineteenth century gave a pattern to some of the anxieties which distressed an urban society "fresh from the country."

In the conventions of this popular literature the "country" was an ambiguous and persistent symbol. Almost invariably, country people had abundant faith and crude manners. The country offered a sanctuary for homespun heroes and heroines who shunned or were ignorant of fashion, parties, and skepticism. The sanctuary was not inviolable, however, and sometimes only a determined, pious death saved the unwary rustic from worldly contamination. The vulnerability of the country was everywhere apparent: in the contempt of the worldly for rural simplicity, in the easy seductions of country maidens by city rakes, in the bumbling shyness of the most virtuous before the urbane.[9]

The city was the resort of the wealthy, the powerful, and the vicious; young men yielded to its glamor until converted by the helpless beauty of a country girl, the pious necessities of a widowed mother, or the nobility of an aged pastor. Transplanted to the city, the rural heroine had limited alternatives: she might die a martyr's death, save her husband, or, briefly seduced by frivolity, she might attend balls, eventually to die, repentant and lost.[10] The dramatic antagonism was rigid; one pole of experience or the other had to collapse.

Yet, within the convention, the country had its own strength, derived from devotion to God and the presence of Nature. Simple piety, busy with the duties of farm and family, could charm even urban depravity. A debutante was disappointed in her return to the city, for she found "something in all this gorgeousness and festivity . . . *unholy*. I have lived so much, of late years, in the wild dells and solemn forests of the country." In the country, sudden religious conviction seized skeptical city dwellers. A backwoods minister, preaching to a member of a fashionable urban church, opened the "avenue of feeling, long sealed by inveterate worldliness."[11]

Though in literary convention piety always preferred the homespun simplicity of country cottages, quilting bees, and church-going, religious men actually proved less bucolic in their choices. Few were willing to accept the dire alternatives of the literary annuals. *The Young Lady's Own Book*, lamenting that the vulgarity of religious people had made piety seem inelegant, urged believers to take more pains for their manners.[12] Ambitious young men could not afford to blunder. From Andover Theological Seminary, the devout Calvinist Joel Hawes cautioned his fiancée to avoid domesticity. "I am afraid of the kitchen. That refinement of taste, delicacy of feeling, and elegance of manners, which I delight to see in others, though I do not possess them myself, cannot be acquired but by being conversant with elegant authors and people of cultivated minds."[13]

Young Bronson Alcott returned from Cheshire Academy convinced that his classmates were ridiculing his homespun and his dialect; later he made the South a school of manners, returning to his native Spindle Hill with debts, the most fashionable coat he could find on Broadway, and the gratifying persuasion that his person and diction had acquired elegance. Rural simplicity had its disadvantages, and religious writers warned that theological students, cloistered with each other and their professors, might graduate boors, unfit to mingle with their polite parishioners.[14]

Gift books vainly protested that "true manners" and piety were indistinguishable; their stories betrayed a different persuasion. No one seemed certain how vast a destruction the existence of polite society might bring to manners and morals, but, outside fiction, few young men making city careers could neglect its sanctions.

Upon graduation from Yale, Bushnell assiduously set about entering the society of Norwich, Connecticut, where he was unenthusiastically teaching school. "I hardly know whether you will believe me," he gaily informed former classmate Cortlandt Van Rensselaer, "but it is a fact, that I have lately taken . . . to visiting the ladies." His mother noted his care to "convert himself into a gentleman" with anxious inquiry after his religion.[15] Yet even after his conversion in 1831, Bushnell urged upon his former Yale students the "importance of polished conciliatory manners," before he apologetically mentioned an "unwelcome subject"—his belief in human immortality and accountability.[16]

Like the homespun, the rocky soil, and the dialects of the country, traditional religious language was linked to a past which mobile men were leaving behind them; by 1851 Bushnell had come to explicit recognition of the distance between the "age of homespun" and his own society. "There was a rigor in their piety, a want of gentle feeling. . . . The mothers of the homespun age had a severe limit on their culture and accomplishments. . . . We demand a delicacy and elegance of manners impossible to them."[17]

Yet neither Bushnell nor his society was ready to dismiss the past to which they were bound by loyalty, love, and respect. The pervasive concern for religion which ran through popular periodicals and many best-sellers demanded

9

the redefinition, not the abolition, of religion. Ambitious, gifted, and conscientious, Bushnell was caught between the time's faith and its condescensions. He knew firsthand the need for religious redefinition, and during the long process of his inquiry, the search for language and a tenable faith fused with the struggle for success and for peace with his origins. With *God in Christ* in 1849, he experienced the relief of resolution.

But the young graduate of Yale College could envisage no such victory. His future career and his chances for success seemed as vague as his faith. Six years after graduation he had judged himself a failure as a schoolteacher and had found New York journalism distasteful. Nonetheless, he did not consider the ministry. He dreamed of political distinction and felt the pressure of time. Having studied the law for six months, he was so anxious to embark on a legal-political career in the West that he unhesitatingly turned down a tutorship at Yale. Only his mother's firm conviction that he should accept the position changed his plans. With the tutorship he combined study in the Yale Law School.

By 1831 Bushnell had completed his law examinations; throughout the two years of tutorship, he experienced difficulty in leading college prayers, and he had communicated his doubts to his students. When a revival swept Yale in 1831, Bushnell and a group of his followers remained aloof. In the chapel and in private talks Professors Goodrich and Fitch demanded that the students choose between conversion and godlessness. Evenings, Nathaniel Taylor preached in the Rhetorical Chambers. The tutors established a religious meeting of their own, but Bushnell did not attend.

The revival and his students' dependence nonetheless sharpened Bushnell's religious anxiety. He felt the need of religious affirmation. Perhaps it was his defection from faith or the felt responsibility for his students' apathy, but cer-

tainly it was some conviction of guilt more assessable than
the despair of total depravity that resulted in the decision
which he called conversion. In this crisis he decided that he
had failed to be ruled by the law of right and that henceforward he would obey that law.

If piety had waned in America, a moral code remained
to assure the skeptic. Besieged by doubts, Bushnell found
he could rely on one certainty: the distinction between
right and wrong. Starting with this moral conviction, by
means of moral choice he tried to cut a path to God. "If
there is a God, . . . he is a right God. If I have lost him in
the wrong, perhaps I shall find him in the right." He prayed
to the "dim God, dimly felt" and was "borne up into God's
help. . . . After this all troublesome doubt of God's reality
is gone."[18] The sinner's anguished need for justification had
been lost in the search for belief. To have won belief in God
and self was salvation.

Beginning with the assumption of man's powers of righteousness, Bushnell could not conceive a God so demanding
or alien that the will had to be broken. For Bushnell, neither
Edwards' ecstatic consent to the inscrutable will of God
nor the "willingness to be damned for the glory of God"
which had tested New Light converts made sense. The
rationale behind the "hard points" of Calvinism had not
troubled him; he had assumed a goodness able to choose
the right and a God so gratified by the decision that the
choice entailed salvation.

Yet if Bushnell's conversion reflected the moralistic Calvinism of his time, he himself thought of faith as the choice
of the heart over the head. Longing for the Trinity which
his reason denied, he determined to "hold" by his heart.[19]
Faith seemed to require the sacrifice of the reason, and the
crucial separation of mind and emotions entered Bushnell's
religious perspective. If Christian belief could be attained

11

only through the feelings and by the denial of reason, theological rationales were redundant. The mind had to be perpetually humbled in the interest of faith and "the heart."

Bushnell had chosen faith, and he quickly fixed upon a ministerial career. He entered the Yale Divinity School in 1831, with no theology and a minimal belief. The prospect must have appeared treacherous to a conscientious man so deeply committed and so flimsily equipped.

II. A Christianity for Common Sense

When Bushnell began his theological studies in 1831, Nathaniel Taylor had ruled the Yale Divinity School for nine years. Taylor's colleagues shared his peculiar views and echoed them in lectures, sermons, and lengthy articles in the *Christian Spectator*. But Taylor himself assumed the burden of presenting the students with the comprehensive, logical *summa* of the course. In the tidy, unhurried hand of S. W. Dutton, a student in 1838, Taylor's ordered syllogisms still remain, unmolested by comments and abundantly underlined. Yet, though pure reason marshaled the notes, Dutton, like his contemporaries, paid tribute to alien gods. Carefully pasted on the notebook cover, the mournful strains of Mrs. Lydia Huntley Sigourney's "Widow's Charge at Her Daughter's Funeral" challenged the austere sequences of logic.

Students could leave the Divinity School secure in the possession of the rationale of God's moral government and trained in the techniques of successful revivalism. Bushnell nonetheless failed to find there the theology his experience demanded. Taylor remembered the student for his belligerent opposition; Bushnell's later praise for his teacher was that Taylor had taught him to think for himself.[1] But in spite of his cherished revolt Bushnell called upon the New Divinity's basic concepts in later life, and he could not escape any more than Taylor had from the context in which Taylor's theology was devised.

13

Taylor's first course, in Mental and Moral Philosophy, reviewed material familiar to most college students. For the course was based upon the common sense realism of Reid, Stewart, Brown, Blair, and Kames, which was standard undergraduate fare in contemporary colleges in America. By the eighteen-thirties, the Scottish common-sense philosophy seemed obvious; for most Americans it determined the limits of sensible doubt and definitively described the human mind. To American delight, it was an empirical philosophy that yet salvaged morality, the existence of things, and the power of the mind to know absolute truth.

The Scottish tradition was empirical in tracing most of man's knowledge to percepts of the mental and material world. As separate images and emotions impinged on the mind, they eventually were linked together by repeated co-existence. Once custom had established linkages between percepts, particular sensations initiated the habitual chain of images and feelings, which eventuated in aesthetic pleasure, intellectual conviction, an emotion, or all three. Thus the past became the key to present belief, and education emerged as the decisive factor in determining mind and character. American gift books, articles, and poetry echoed the theory that experience joined ideas and feelings in irrevocable union; plastic, ductile, the creature of the past, the "mind" had been brought into clear focus and confronted parents and reformers, politicians and ministers.

Even more gratifying than the educational susceptibilities of the mind described by Scottish realism was its ability to achieve the truth. Though the realists disputed the number and content of self-evident truths, they agreed that the mind did possess incontestable intuitions. As Taylor taught, the instrument of such felicitous certainties was common sense, or "the reason of mankind generally . . . employed in making those decisions which it is competent to make, arriving of course at uniform and infallible decisions."[2]

If the definition was circular, the assurance was agreeable though not startling to Americans. Self-consciously proving the success of the democratic experiment to antiquated old world monarchies, Americans were accustomed to recognize their own competence. The arcanum of political science had proved transparent to republican vision; before an attentive world the common man was demonstrating his mastery of the art and theory of self-government. And revolutionary confidence flourished with the decades. Throughout the nineteenth century, state constitutions were revised to abolish property requirements for suffrage; in 1840 Whigs and Democrats noisily vied in their praise of the common man. Foreigners occasionally found the national complacency oppressive. In 1833 Thomas Hamilton noted that Americans treated intricate problems as so obvious that any schoolboy could easily decide them. "The Americans seem to imagine themselves imbued with the power of *feeling* truth." The persuasion that the individual mind could settle every issue seemed to De Tocqueville to be the universal philosophical assumption of Americans.[3]

American self-assurance did not spare theology, which, De Tocqueville reported, reigned less "as a doctrine of revelation than as a commonly received opinion."[4] In the democracy of belief a learned elite could not command assent because of trained or superior understanding. As the *New Englander* warned, the proper test of religious doctrine was not the "opinion of philosophers" but the untrained judgment of the "mass of men."[5] Measured by common sense, theological truth was as discernible to the layman as to the cleric, and Taylor's New Divinity proposed to the public "not a dark hall full of mysteries, but *terra firma* covered with light; and not mere speculation and vain philosophy,

15

but the main-spring, . . . sinews, and muscle of revival preaching."[6]

American ministers seized upon the common-sense philosophy with an avidity that betrayed their need. Conscious of the victories of Unitarians in Massachusetts and of Episcopalians in Connecticut, New England Calvinists were prepared to muffle some of the orthodox doctrines which offended contemporary American common sense. In Calvinism the inscrutable decrees of God—damnation of the many, the election of some to unmerited salvation, the "offense" of the Cross—had rested at a point of transcendent mystery and were known only by revelation. Yet nineteenth-century articles on homiletics enthused at the singular compatibility of Christianity and common sense; eventually, the *New Englander* praised the democratic facility of Christian belief. Christianity had such "few and plain" essential doctrines that the lowest classes could understand it "very early in life." It was happily a "strong system," "cheaply received, cheaply supported, and cheaply propagated."[7]

Clerical methods, too, had to be revised for successful encounters with republican common sense. Religious periodicals warned that it was futile to rely on the voluminous logic of eighteenth-century divines. No one would accept a conclusion "repugnant" to his intuitions anyway. However flawless the reasoning, Ebenezer Porter warned, "any plain man" would "boldly pronounce" a conclusion false if it offended his innate certainties.[8]

Of all the self-evident principles of the mind, moral truths seemed to Americans the most obvious and the most precious. Like the Scottish realists, Taylor taught that the principles of moral obligation were absolute cognitions that did not depend on reason or experience. A heritage of eighteenth-century rationalism, the conviction that the human

16

mind universally possessed the law of right was shared by Old and New School Calvinists, Unitarians, Quakers, and deists. Though Paul had declared that without the revealed law he had not known sin, and though both Paul and Luther had announced that faith not virtue was the antithesis of sin, Americans were convinced that the reason knew the law of virtue, that the will was obliged by it, and that sin was the failure to observe it. As Timothy Dwight announced to Yale seniors, virtue was "nothing but voluntary obedience to truth; and Sin nothing but voluntary obedience to falsehood."[9]

This structure of universal moral obligation, binding upon God and man, became the basis of New England theology and of Taylor's New Divinity. By the time of the Revolution it had become obvious that honorable men could not give allegiance to a Deity beyond the law, whimsically dispensing condemnations or pardons. The political metaphor, within which God functioned as a ruler earning his subjects' loyalty by a judicious benevolence, captured the imagination of the post-Revolutionary generations and sounded through the writings of the younger Edwards, Dwight, Emmons, Bellamy, and Taylor.

Taylor's New Divinity rested upon the epistemology and the ethical absolutism of the Scottish common-sense philosophy. Nonetheless, it was radical enough to make New Haven the center of religious controversies for over a decade. Though the passionate debate, which circled around Taylor's peculiar doctrines on evil, moral agency, and regeneration, was tedious to the student Bushnell, he learned his lessons well enough to incorporate many of Taylor's concepts in his own theology.

Designed for efficient preaching and the defeat of Unitarianism, Taylor's theology bore the marks of popular preferences. At every point the power of God was limited to make Him reasonable, just, and acceptable to man. The world was so dominated by His benevolence that His nature was crossed and thwarted by sin. He had permitted evil in the world not wilfully but because the world with its evil was the best alternative available to His choice, and He offered for man's approval the best of all possible universes.

Under God's benign administration, happiness was good and suffering was evil. Since all men sought their own happiness, self-interest was divinely sanctioned. Thus God's just equation of human nature and moral duty made man's obligation and pleasure alike the blithe pursuit of happiness. Sin was only the error that happiness and selfishness were identical. Thus defined as folly, sin called less for reprobation than enlightenment, and through the scourges of natural evil God pressed upon erring man the recognition that he had won not happiness but pain. Under this vigorous and salutary discipline, the faltering creature was led toward salvation.

The Unitarian protest had harped relentlessly on Calvinism's damnation of doomed and helpless human beings. In concerted strategy, Taylor and Beecher outlined a gentler orthodoxy that exonerated God and encouraged man by insisting on the possibility of human righteousness. Man was a moral neuter, without sin until he violated the law of right, a simple idea intuitively perceived and universally accepted. Though certain to sin, he had "power to the contrary"; the decision and the guilt were his own.

Primarily seeking a Calvinism which could be preached effectively, Taylor argued that neither the minister nor the sinner should be discouraged by the fact of depravity. For the preacher had only to appeal to the "neutral" self-love at the core of the personality and to demonstrate to man that his true happiness lay in obedience to God's law. Thus enlightened, the sinner could be freed from his bondage to selfishness. Such a saving change demanded none of the desperate, probing scrutiny by self and community which the early Puritans had required. It could come with gratifying swiftness and transform the sinner into the saint. That men "*must* suffer pangs and glooms for years, that they *must* go through the . . . protracted process of law-work," had become an antiquated notion, according to the *Christian Spectator*.[10]

By the time Bushnell entered Divinity School, the earlier Calvinism of New England had been transformed to meet the requirements of republican common sense. The terrible *deus absconditus* of Calvinism had become genial, rational, and reliable. Under the epistemology of common-sense realism, God and man were bound together by mutual perception and acknowledgment of the right. Republicans could easily revere a God who had made man so susceptible to salvation and who aimed only at good government and human felicity. The New Divinity became Bushnell's point of departure. He never lost the conviction of the overwhelming benevolence of God or the sense of intimate moral kinship between God and man. Like Taylor, he worked for conversions that would turn the will from selfishness to love.

The student nonetheless passed through the course persistently disavowing all discipleship. The very questions that inspired passionate controversies throughout New England were rejected. Bushnell chose to enter the ministry without the reassurance of an authoritative system of divinity. His choice meant that he would have to define his position piecemeal while his people scrutinized his sermons, alert for the heresies of Taylorism or the outmoded orthodoxy of Tylerism, while they watched and waited for a "season of refreshment" or for the untoward enthusiasm that might vulgarize the scene.

Bushnell's aggressive, costly rejection was inspired not by

19

orthodox loyalties but by imperative personal experiences which were still unrationalized and inarticulate. Taylor's methods and questions only continued the traditions of rural religious thought. Building upon the familiar idiom of the New England theology, Taylor offered no way to address a society which feared the marks of its own past. Just as Bushnell had not lost his faith because of perplexities about evil or free agency, he was not reassured by Taylor's resolution of these problems. Bushnell's New Preston pastor had repeatedly pondered God's wisdom in the permission of sin; Bushnell himself was ready to drop the question. He knew by his own experience that religion had not fallen out of fashion because men felt doomed to sin and suffer. The theology of common sense did not answer the needs of those who had held to religion by the heart. Though Bushnell had been converted again, he did not want to return to the methods of his childhood faith; the profound unsettlement of his college years lay behind his irritated certainty that Taylor's system was inappropriate and sterile.

But if the cause of the rejection lay in Bushnell's past, the rejection itself was prophetic. He had already acquired the focus of that religious sensibility which would eventually transform the Calvinism of common sense. In the long, arduous search for a new language and a different perspective, Bushnell found his first ally in Samuel Taylor Coleridge, whose writings would assuage and emancipate other young men from the country who descended upon Boston with "knives in their brains."[11]

III. The Preferences of the
Romantic Sensibility

Unimpressed by Taylor's elaborate rationale of God's moral government and weary of the familiar idiom of his New Preston church, Bushnell suddenly discovered in the *Aids to Reflection* an escape from his hostile isolation. As an old man, Bushnell testified that he owed more to the *Aids* than to any other book except the Bible. The praise casts strong light upon the extremity and gratification of the student, for Bushnell never admitted intellectual debts easily. Coleridge somehow addressed the perplexed faith which Taylor had failed to satisfy.

Between 1830 and 1850 many theological students experienced a similar excitement on reading the *Aids*. First published in America in 1829 by James Marsh of the University of Vermont, the *Aids to Reflection* met errant religious needs among students whose professors recommended and expounded Paley, Butler, Edwards, Taylor, or their own "systems of divinity." In 1842 Emerson noted that at Andover the *Aids* sold by the "shelvesful," while throughout the thirties and forties standard religious periodicals testified to Coleridge's appeal by lengthy refutations or occasional praise. By 1848 the *Princeton Review* sorrowfully conceded that Coleridge had a "strong moulding influence" upon "a certain class of minds."[1]

In contrast to Taylorite Divinity, Coleridge admitted the difficulties of sophisticated belief. "Never be afraid to doubt," the *Aids* counseled, "if only you have the disposition to believe, and doubt in order that you may end in believing the truth."[2] The book did not proceed by syllogisms; learned, diffuse, eclectic, the *Aids* moved fitfully, passing from Kantian theorizing to exhortation, pausing to lambast Paley or the present age, yet throughout its apparent disorder communicating a curious, ardent faith.

The method of the *Aids* was in itself an emancipation to Americans. In place of premises and conclusions, aphorisms and "comments" invited the reader to ponder, dispute, or assent. The freewheeling procedure was agreeable to American students who had failed to be persuaded by marshaled logic. The *Aids* offered a new model of preaching to the younger clergy. Eventually, contemporary reviewers would praise Bushnell for his sudden insights and elliptical reasoning or would blame him for his indifference to logical order.[3]

In spite of its disjunctive style, the *Aids* offered a coherent interpretation of religion, based on a Kantian rather than an empirical epistemology. Coleridge had found a structure for his faith in Kant's differentiation between the Reason and the Understanding, and Marsh's Preface announced that this distinction was essential to the book. The Understanding was the faculty that related and gave form to sensations. Yet, despite these services, the Understanding was an unreliable instrument of knowledge. Dependent upon the senses for all its materials, the Understanding abstracted, generalized, named, and compared. It had no independent authority and brought no immediate truths. The Understanding constructed theological systems but knew nothing of spiritual experience; it functioned only in the realm of nature which the spirit transcended. The "hollowness and tricksy sophistry" of "Natural Theology" resulted from the misguided use of the Understanding. For "wherever the forms of reasoning appropriate only to the *natural* world are applied to *spiritual* realities, . . . the more strictly logical the reasoning is in all its *parts*, the more irrational it is as a *whole*." The logical pyramid of Taylor's lectures, which built upon man's sensations, self-interest, and common sense, toppled easily for converts to this new epistemology.

But if the Understanding was spiritually blind, man still had access to uncontingent spiritual truths. The Reason beheld the truth directly, "having a similar relation to the Intelligible or Spiritual as sense has to the Material or Phenomenal."[4] The Reason was autonomous; it did not depend upon sensations or the restricting forms of space and time but permitted transcendent knowledge of moral law and spiritual existence.

Instead of restricting experience to the harmonious interplay of sensations and common sense, the *Aids* thus depicted two worlds in which man might function: the Understanding's orbit of nature and the Reason's realm of conscience and insight. The gap between the phenomenal and the spiritual universes might prove ethically painful and intellectually frustrating, but it made sense to Americans torn between the requirements of the head and the heart.

Like Scottish common sense, the Reason guaranteed the validity of the insights it bestowed, but to the penetrating mind it brought a richer promise. The seeker after spiritual discernment was no longer constrained within the limits of universal consent. Certainty did not need to wait upon general agreement but was born in the sudden impact of personal vision. The individual who felt at odds with his time or tradition might hope for truth; such an emancipation from Unitarian or Calvinist orthodoxy was welcome to many Americans, as it was to the young Bushnell. Though the *Aids* did not probe the methods of distinguishing truth from subjective delusions, Coleridge's American disciples were not disturbed; they had long been more oppressed by the need for escape than by any ambitions for flawless logic.

Yet just because the apprehensions of the Reason were not simple and obvious, the seer faced the isolation of eccentric private enthusiasms. Consisting in revelations to the individual and describing visions distant from the common world of ordered sense experience, the Reason's religious knowledge might be only the private dreams of countless recalcitrant hearts. Like the transcendentalists, Bushnell in following Coleridge risked subjectivism; like them, he would try to tie his lofty visions to an objective, shared reality.

Here, too, Coleridge pointed the way. Cryptically the *Aids* suggested that a "thing, power, or principle" could be expressed by the "same thing, power, or principle in a lower, but more known form." Simple, common language had carried and still could carry the transcendent perceptions of the Reason. Americans who found contemporary theological conventions unpersuasive and archaic welcomed the hope that ordinary words could convey the deepest insights of the spirit. Baffled by much of the book, Bushnell fastened on Coleridge's brief, scattered hints about language. To the young, country-bred man who at college had discovered that he had no suitable language, Coleridge's doctrine promised escape from provincial oddity and spiritual isolation. For here, as he enthusiastically testified, he found that "language built on physical images is itself two stories high, and is, in fact, an outfit for a double range of uses."[5]

But for the most part, the *Aids*, like the majority of Americans, was less concerned with language than with morals and religion. Coleridge based ethics in an absolute apprehension, "without reference to space or time or sensible existence."[6] Man's moral existence did not consist in the exercise of self-interest. Scorning the "mechanical self-love" scheme of Paley, Coleridge announced that morality was founded not in prudence but in uncompromising law. In the moral act man was free, and his obedience sprang from his delighted acknowledgment of his duty.

Coleridge was anxious to establish the supremacy of the moral law, and his reasoning followed Kant's. The Reason perceived the ideas that were the necessary premises of the moral life, and the conscience enjoined belief in these ideas, without which it itself would be a contradiction. Those premises and conclusions essential to morality needed no further proof. Primary among them was the freedom of the will, for, if conscience was to have validity, man had to be able to do that which conscience commanded. The capacity and proper allegiance of the will distinguished man from things. Self-originative, above the operations of cause and effect, the will was the supernatural element in man, which separated him from the interdependent sequences of the natural world.

The concern for human freedom was a familiar one to Americans, whether they had been trained in the orthodoxy of Jonathan Edwards, the "improvements" of Taylor, or the Arminianism of Unitarians. Americans, too, shared Coleridge's mistrust of the mechanical operations of self-love. In New England, where Edwardsean converts had achieved a selfless love for Being in general and Hopkinsians had been willing to be damned for the glory of God, the higgling morality of self-interest seemed poor measure of man's potential grandeur. The transcendent ethic of Coleridge restored obligation to a plane where disinterested benevolence could once again press its excessive but flattering requirements upon the human conscience. Yet if the *Aids* permitted an exhilarating conviction of a uniquely human dignity, the book performed a further service for students and professors committed to orthodoxy. For Coleridge held that the will was essentially corrupt. By an originative act of freedom, outside space and time, the will in some inexplicable election had chosen evil. This act of freedom, mythically represented in the fall of Adam and Eve, characterized all human experience. Man was involved in contradictions, "a mysterious diversity between the injunctions of the mind and the elections of the will."[7] From his decisive apostasy no man could save himself, though the book stated that Christ's example might somehow be redeeming.

Coleridge offered a new vocabulary when established modes of expressions seemed inadequate; "Reason," the "supernatural," "subjective," "elections of the will," usurped the place of "self-interest," "common sense," "moral government," "pleasures and pains." Centering on questions different from those of the New England tradition, and justifying belief through an esoteric epistemology, the *Aids* mediated escape from worn theological controversies. The release was the more intoxicating in that the ideas were largely pre-empted without the epistemological structure behind them. In his preface to the *Aids*, Marsh did not explore the grounds of the distinction between the Reason and the Understanding but attacked the American tendency to neglect the spiritual life in favor of speculative theology. Most of Coleridge's American disciples were more delighted by the disparity between the mechanical Understanding and the intuitive Reason than by the analysis which defined the limits of each. William G. T. Shedd, who taught at Andover and Union, explained Kant's Pure Reason to students as essentially "the open, unbiased nature of childhood."[8]

There is no evidence that Bushnell turned to Kant for better understanding of Coleridge. He trusted to his own experience for the tools of comprehension. What he seized upon as crucial and how he interpreted it were determined by his personal needs and by the American situation which pressed its own questions and its own vocabulary upon him.

Even before Coleridge made any sense to him, Bushnell had decided to hold to Christianity by the heart, and he read Coleridge through the lens of an emerging American romanticism. Coleridge provided a sophisticated rationale for preferences made pervasive, proper, and almost imperative by urban middle-class literature. The romanticism of the gift books, popular novels, and poetry of contemporary America shaped Bushnell's vocabulary and imagination more decisively than did the metaphysics of the *Aids*.

Wandering in Europe, contemplating man and divinity in his Hartford study, or planning a city park, Bushnell formulated his experience through the categories familiar to this middle-class literature: the "sublime," the "infinite," the "heart," the "heroic." In isolation, a "sweet sense of estrangement" crept over him, and he responded to the "sublime cataracts" of the East Hampton ocean and of Niagara as to the "divine music" which he heard in "the lofty passes of the Alps." In spite of his militant anti-Catholicism and anti-Puseyism, he was continually "dissolved in feeling" in Gothic churches and at Anglican and Catholic services in Europe. On the Continent his thoughts circled around the heroic figure of Napoleon; in his sermons he exalted "something far beyond" the mere "dignity of human nature"—"a wild strange flame raging inwardly in that nature."[9] As he praised the demonic wildness in man's nature, so he found the spontaneous play of virtuous impulses nobler than a rational control. He did not share Kant's conviction that man acted righteously only in the conquest of desire by conscience; for Bushnell, virtue was the "play" of the soul, in which inclination and duty merged.

Bushnell's task became the revision of American Protestantism in terms of the *Aids'* transcendentalism and of American romanticism. It was not an easy job. As Nietzsche would point out, the romantic ethos that made Napoleon a hero made Christ the prophet of a slave morality. The romantic exaltation of impulse and passion took no account of the Pauline conflict between the flesh and the spirit or of the required Christian discipline of the natural man. Romantic methodology threatened the whole deposit of faith, for the lonely discoveries of individual insight bypassed Christian tradition and revelation.[10] These tensions between traditional Christianity and nineteenth-century romanticism played through Bushnell's religious thought, and much of his achievement lay in his complex mediation between two realms of value.

In thus formulating Christianity in a mode that answered the needs of the heart, Bushnell made extensive though partial use of the *Aids*. If the Reason, guilty by association of the logic-splitting techniques of New England divines, had no function in Bushnell's theology, the Understanding provided a fixed point of reference and value. It was the measuring, quantitative faculty, the source of metaphysics, theological systems, and picayune distinctions. To the reviled Understanding, Bushnell consistently opposed not the Reason but the heart.

The law of right and the powers of a moral agent were familiar to any New England college student. But Coleridge gave man a heroic stature based on the will which made him a "living power." For Bushnell, it was here, in the antithesis between the moral law and human nature, in the contempt for self-love as the route to sanctity, that Coleridge most gratifyingly challenged the New Divinity.

In one of the earliest of his remaining papers, written in 1832, Bushnell attacked the self-love scheme. Yet even the attack revealed Taylor's power more than Coleridge's. The scrupulous definition of terms, the arrangement of premises and conclusions, the battery of argument, derive from his professor; more significantly, so do his major premises—that every man has a conviction of duty and is governed by self-love, that a moral act is a choice between goods, and that duty and happiness are identical. Using Taylor's methods and assumptions, Bushnell arrived at the triumphant conclusion that since man did sin, he was involved in a self-contradiction which no philosophy could resolve. The victorious air of the paper conveys the complacency of the student who has outwitted his professor; the defeat of Taylor's reasoning seemed proof of the defeat of all reason before the mystery of man.

At one point Bushnell found Taylor vulnerable. Neither the corruption of man nor the power of the Cross was at the center of his critique, but a vision of human grandeur. In the self-love system the glory of man as sinner or saint had been lost. Taylor had failed to account for the sublimity of a Napoleon. "Why sin is so rugged a conflict within he does not inquire, that wonderful power by virtue of which he frustrates the laws and ends of his being he does not see."[11] Beyond the reach of cause, the will was the mark of man's divinity.

In 1833 Bushnell received a call from the North Church of Hartford. Within the same year he married Mary Apthorp. With his increased responsibilities, he forfeited the role of student-critic. He had now to enlighten and convert his people and their children, to strengthen his church, and to formulate his position and aims as a Christian minister. Two generations earlier, Dwight, Emmons, and Hopkins had resolved these problems by preaching systems of divinity; in the more recent past, Lyman Beecher and Charles Finney had achieved fame and success through revivals. Bushnell neither possessed nor believed in systems of divinity, and he had rejected the theories with which Taylor, Beecher, and Finney had launched into effective revivalism. His ambition was to become a professor of moral philosophy.[12] But he had first to make himself known.

His techniques would be determined within a social context he could not control. The society he would encounter, like that which he had known, would be impelled toward intellectual assent by a non-rational complex of interests and loyalties. Bushnell's own experience had taught him that Taylor's logic could not persuade the contemporary imagination. Yet, like Taylor, he had to face and conquer the modern audience with its republican self-confidence, its sentimental susceptibilities, its ambivalence toward its own traditions. He had to find a language that could bridge the gap between two societies and to work out a divinity accommodated to American sensibility.

Bushnell did not approach this society with Machiavellian detachment; to a great extent its preferences, tastes, and confusions were his own. He had felt firsthand the pressure of the society's mixed commitments; they had become a part of his personality and conviction. Necessarily, because he was human, the forces which operated upon his beliefs had not been exclusively intellectual. He had been affected by his own past and by the aesthetic and emotional preferences that foreran and determined the "rationality" of premises.

Nonetheless, in the last analysis, Bushnell's resolution of the perplexed religious situation would be rationalized and systematic. The Scottish philosophy, the New Divinity, the *Aids to Reflection*, the inclinations of romanticism, provided the intellectual material from which he would draw throughout his life. If his lack of structured theology made him the more susceptible to contemporary pressures, his ambition and his vulnerability were coupled with an unremitting quest for intellectual integrity.

30

IV. A Fastidious People

In 1833 the young minister and his wife settled in Hartford, staying in the home of one of the church deacons until the parsonage was ready. The city, as Samuel Goodrich recalled it, was "a small commercial town . . . dealing in lumber and smelling of molasses and old Jamaica, . . . strongly impressed with a plodding, mercantile, and mechanical character." Among the "few merchants and many shop-keepers" some "dainty patricians still held themselves aloof."[1] Etchings and pictures of Hartford in the thirties viewed the city from the river, setting buildings and church spires at a picturesque distance. The city lived by the trade which flowed up and down the Connecticut River, and private wharves lined the waterfront. Steamboats transported passengers between Hartford and Springfield and collected Indian corn and lumber from the hinterland.

From the first, Bushnell's situation linked him closely with the mercantile interests of the town, for his new church was dominated by prominent merchants and retailers. Inevitably his career would fluctuate with the shifts in their prosperity; inevitably he would come to know their perspective, their ethos, and their power. Historically, his vocation obliged him to instruct these men in the Christian pursuit of their labors, to call them to repentance and salvation, and to teach them the Gospel. Practically, his task was even more difficult. At a time of frequent changes in church membership, he had to hold the church together; with the demeanor and vocabulary learned in the country, at Yale College, and Yale Divinity School, he had to win the attention and approval of Hartford's "better" classes. During his novitiate Bushnell could be certain that his ability would be measured against that of his predecessors and colleagues and that his failures would be tabulated by empty pews. Thirty-two years old, already rejected by several churches,[2] with a wife to support, he could not afford to lose his pastorate or watch it dwindle in prestige, wealth, or numbers. His position bound him to the financial and social elite who dominated his church, and in this taut connection he found both constraints and illuminations. The society he closely knew and had to please stamped its mark upon all his work.

During the early nineteenth century, Hartford capitalists chiefly invested in commerce, banding together locally to insure their cargoes against destruction. Yet commercial plans were often thwarted, and the unstable economy of trade helped shape Bushnell's conception of Christian enterprise. In the thirties a line of rotting docks along the river reminded passers-by of the too sanguine expectations of West Indies traders. With the opening of steamboat traffic, the local *Courant* envisaged a Hartford emporium tapping the wealth of South America, and the Connecticut River Banking and Steamboat Company was formed to exploit the river trade up to Vermont with Hartford steamboats. But the expansive vision of investors was shattered by the opening of the Boston and Springfield Railroad, which cut Hartford from northern New England. Capitalists next pinned their hopes on railroads, but though Hartford and New Haven were connected by rail in 1839, and Hartford and Springfield by 1844, trade still lagged. By 1846 the *Courant* dolefully recorded that the city verged on economic ruin.[3]

Though small factories and domestic industries eased the financial strain of the mid-century, the city's economic future was uncertain during most of Bushnell's pastorate. Throughout the early nineteenth century the *Courant* deplored the tendency of Hartford businessmen to invest their capital outside the city.[4] Falling real estate values, lack of trade, and unemployment in the 1840's brought fear and schemes for improvement. Mindful of the success of Lowell, merchants proposed that the water of Windsor Locks be piped to supply power for Hartford. Bushnell joined in the promotion, addressing the city's businessmen on the religious duty of economic progress and the moral peril of failure. Yet, despite the exigencies of religion and prosperity, the plan came to nothing.

The Hartford merchant knew he held his wealth in precarious tenure. The town had witnessed the melancholy withdrawal of the Charles Sigourneys from the spacious lawns and high-columned mansion of their estate to a city house too small to admit their "massy side-board" or the "alabaster ornaments" which had graced their mantel. In 1819 Thomas Brace resigned from the presidency of the Aetna Fire Insurance Company because of "pecuniary embarrassments," and in mid-century, citizens whispered that William Imlay, once one of the two wealthiest men in Hartford, was hard pressed for money.[5]

Yet, despite personal reverses, a steady, select group of citizens largely controlled the wealth of Hartford and prospered in the face of obstacles. Capital localized increasingly in insurance companies, which by the mid-fifties carried policies all over the nation, and in banks, which had a total capital of over $4,000,000. Pictures of Hartford at mid-century focused on the business streets, portraying a few carriages parked outside the stocky stone respectability of the Phoenix or Hartford Insurance Companies or the principal banks. Year after year, listing the officers of the major financial institutions, the city directory repeated the same names. When the Aetna Life Insurance Company was formed, stockholders of the Aetna Fire Insurance Company subscribed the total capital. Thus strategically located, the financial aristocracy of Hartford was never embarrassed by lack of capital, and bank commissioners reported that no debts were of "such long continuance and perpetual renewal as the debts of directors."[6]

Hartford willingly recognized its own patricians and elected Seth Terry, Amos Collins, James Hosmer, Thomas Brace, and their peers to serve as mayors, committeemen, or justices of the peace. Contemporary accounts reveal the city's consciousness of its aristocracy. Early in the nineteenth century the best families sponsored Assembly Balls, where dancing continued until two but card-playing was prohibited. After her impressive marriage Lydia Sigourney, poetess and former schoolmistress, boasted of "marked regard from the aristocracy," but in spite of such condescension she remained diffident in social gatherings.[7] And Joel Hawes, pastor of the First Church, found in Hartford a "less familiar courtesy [than in Boston] and an apparent coldness," detecting a "negative quality in almost everybody." The ladies in Hawes's church, meanwhile, complained that he spat too freely.[8]

Hartford's first citizens prided themselves on their refinement, their reading, and their responsiveness to Goldsmith.[9] The rector of St. John's Church published *Christian Ballads;* one of Bushnell's parishioners joined gothic horrors with moral maxims in *Tales of Devils and the Supernatural;* and anonymous poems and stories in gift books often bore the simple honorific label, "Hartford, Connecticut." At the center of the city's literary pretensions stood Lydia Sigourney, whose quivering sensibility and religious devotion made her "the American Mrs. Hemans." Mrs. Sigourney set up a "small literary circle" for the edification of the young.[10] Impressed by the city's artistic and intellectual activities, Charles Finney concluded that "no city in the world" was as educated as Hartford, and young Joel Hawes despondently decided that his congregation knew "too much" for him and that he was better suited to "some small country town."[11]

Yet Hartford's upper and middle classes held their aesthetic indulgences under the nervous rein of felt moral duty. A long battle raged over the state law prohibiting theater. In 1837 one thousand Hartford citizens, led by the Episcopal Bishop Brownell, petitioned against the law. Prominent Congregationalists spearheaded the defensive, and the law remained on the books twenty-five years longer, though its enforcement was sporadic. In 1846 the *Religious Herald* cautioned unwary readers against a troupe which was luring citizens into theatricals by the promise of "temperance exhibitions." Only the "moral drama" of *Uncle Tom's Cabin* appeased the suspicions of the pious and was graced by the attendance of "some of the best people of the city" with their "wives and children."[12]

If the theater, shadowed by a dubious past, remained suspect, the lecture room offered more austere opportunities for self-improvement, and Hartford supported the lyceum movement with conscientious aplomb. The *Courant* was delighted to recommend so elevating a substitute for "vicious amusements." After 1849 two local societies serviced the need for information and oratory, and thirty lectures a season invited the curious and the dutiful. Between 1840 and 1856 Hartford audiences listened to Ralph Waldo Emerson, Mark Hopkins, Horace Greeley, Henry Ward Beecher, Thomas Hart Benton; in 1846 Bushnell instructed a meeting

35

at the Young Men's Institute on the disparity between "Taste and Fashion."[13]

Prosperous businessmen bent on culture and morality could be conscious of their own well-doing. The *Courant* carried advertisements for concerts, fairs, rallies, and benefits for the aid of the Cherokees, the Jews, the Greeks, or the Negroes.[14] Subscribers to the Asylum for the Deaf and Dumb and the Hartford Retreat for the Insane were largely Hartford people, and Thomas Gallaudet exulted that Providence had placed deaf-mute Alice Cogswell in Hartford, which had so peculiarly great a supply of the world's "intelligence, enterprise, and benevolence."[15] Ministers chorused the praise of the mercantile classes, which had, according to Joel Hawes, the "greatest part of vital, fruitful piety in the world."[16] Able to find no one "more genuinely Christ-like" than the Christian merchant, Bushnell promised the "morning of a new creation" once the present service of wealth to Christ's kingdom reached its culmination.[17]

The middle-class charities aimed at the salvation of pagans, prisoners, the handicapped, or the benighted by means of religious training. The objects of benevolence were usually remote from the donors, who hoped to redeem their charges by Christian knowledge, not by the transformation of society. Fund-raisers for Gallaudet's work with the deaf and dumb rejoiced primarily that he had made it possible for them to know the Gospel.[18]

The appeal of such charities was complex. The hold of the church was waning, and theology had ceased to interest the public; yet the need to pay some tribute to religion remained imperative. Controlled and maintained by laymen, open to members without requiring any profession of faith, moral societies were voluntary associations not presupposing the minister or the church. There were many, Horace Bushnell remarked, who "would have more pleasure in the communion if it were more select."[19] Furthermore, in the positive testimony of action the converted found a solidity lacking in mere speculation. The New England religious tradition had long identified virtue with benevolence; now men like Finney, Gallaudet, and Bushnell promised that the world would be transformed by the efficient love which was the sign of grace.[20]

Disquietude may have pressed men of business to moral activity. Books, sermons, and articles reiterated, despite nagging uncertainty in laymen and clerics, that business success and Christianity *were* compatible. Doubts protruded in the midst of reassurances. "To look at this man, pushing, driving, bargaining, . . . you would pronounce him decidedly avaricious," conceded the *Princeton Review*, describing the "successful merchant."[21] Even though virtue was benevolence, articles assured the merchant that he could virtuously follow his own interests. Bushnell deplored the idea that trade, "eager and sharp" and tending toward a "mechanical hardness," conflicted with Christianity, and he pointed out that the shrewd merchant could merge profit and benevolence by selling worn, shabby, or leftover goods to the poor at low prices.[22]

Yet no one seemed firmly convinced that religion and trade were complementary. When depressions came, ministers proclaimed the panic a divine judgment against avarice and speculation. Revivals followed close on the heels of business crisis. And even when no hard times accused the prosperous, some merchants seemed to find themselves in an uneasy truce. In the flush of his success Normand Smith, a pious Hartford merchant, felt called to give up his business. Following his pastor's advice, he remained in trade but sought untiringly for services by which he could reaffirm his piety. His journal recorded his uneasiness. "Eternity appears nearer than usual. Many good objects press upon my mind, and I seem impatient to have them done at once." In itself the calling had become inadequate; such men sought from benevolent activity a kind of absolution. Smith foresaw a fine future for the minister who showed him in a "very practical sermon" how he as a merchant "might glorify God probably more than if I were placed in any other situation."[23]

For the most part, Hartford charities were directed at stricken individuals removed from immediate society, and when attention turned to the increasing Irish Catholics or Negroes in the city, the middle classes hoped for a speedy transformation or else despaired. The city's commercial economy had not prepared the prosperous for a large fixed society of poor. During the 1830's, sailors and transients had made the river front the scene of frequent petty crimes, but, in contrast to Boston, Hartford had penalized such miscreants without worrying excessively over their salvation. As canal and railroad construction drew immigrant Irish Catholic laborers, however, the poorer classes gradually took on the shape of a settled society with their own churches, newspapers, pleasures, and reforms. By 1850, with over 3,000 foreign-born in the city, a St. Patrick's Society, a Hibernian Society, and a Catholic temperance group flourished. The Negroes, too, had their own African Free Church, though they were permitted to sit behind screens in some white churches and peer at the service through holes.[24]

Merchants, who had hoped to save heathendom in mass conversions and to abolish ignorance and evil, were baffled by the numerous aliens, who lived in cramped quarters, who listened to their own priests rather than to the pillars of society, and who enjoyed themselves in saloons and billiard halls rather than in parlors. Puzzled and repelled, they ignored the alien population as far as possible, aided in their aloofness by the fact that insurance and banking forced no economic ties between different classes and that the household manufacturing system brought minimal contacts.

Sudden violence occasionally betrayed the latent tensions in the society. In 1834 and 1835 hoodlums plundered the Hartford African Church and wrecked several Negro homes. Halfway through a concert by Jenny Lind, for which tickets had been privately sold, a riot started up in the dense crowd listening from fences and rooftops. The mayor and chief of police, unable to curb the tumult, had to bundle the Swedish Nightingale out of the city.[25]

During the 1840's and 1850's crime increased in the city; the jail capacity doubled. Meanwhile, the balance of political power came to hinge upon the Irish vote. It seemed increasingly difficult to ignore the resident poor, and in 1851 the *Courant* protested the city's apathy, since gambling saloons stood "on every corner" and houses of prostitution bordered the houses of the city's "most respected and influential citizens."[26]

When they attempted to deal with the immediate community, the Protestant middle classes relied primarily upon education, which would train Catholic aliens in democracy and morality, would provide the most able with a chance to leave poverty and strangeness, and would give all classes some knowledge of each other before they settled in the separateness of adult life. Bushnell voiced such hopes, and warned that distinct school systems imperiled the social order of the republic. Private schools nursed "factions, cabals, agrarian laws, and contests of force," he announced in a lecture on "Modifications Demanded by the Roman Catholics" in the schools. Only the common schools, where the poor confronted their own comparative inability or rose to new status, could bring mutual trust and understanding among all classes.[27]

Yet the public schools did not provide the ready, unifying

force Bushnell required. He sent his own children, two daughters and one son, to private schools, while by 1854 almost seven hundred Catholic boys attended St. Patrick's Free School, St. Joseph's School, and the Catholic School. Insisting that a valid, complete education had to be Catholic, rebellious at the school use of the Protestant Bible and the Protestant teaching of history, Catholic leaders did not support Bushnell's common-school program. To many Catholic families in any event the common schools were useless, for, as their Bishop testified, the children worked daily in factories for essential income.[28]

Hartford's upper classes largely left Catholic aliens to their own devices. "Our range of life," Bushnell told his congregation, "is so walled up by the respectability of our associations, that what is on the other side of the wall is very much a world unknown."[29] In 1855 the *Courant* deplored the un-American political power of the priesthood, but saw no remedy but Know-Nothingism.[30] The YMCA, established in 1853, was open only to Protestants.[31] The *Courant* referred to the Irish section of Hartford as "Pigville" and supported the Know-Nothing party in 1855. When the editor shifted to the Republican party, he explained that his position was highly consistent; with Know-Nothingism he had tried to save America from the Irish; with Republicanism he hoped to rescue the nation from "the pestilential presence of the black race."[32]

Bushnell rationalized the prevailing contempt for religious, national, or racial aliens. Blurring distinctions among them, he treated them all with practical neglect and theoretic derogation. Immigration, "infecting and diluting" the British stock, was corrupting the American heritage. The nation's future was safe only because the "uncultivated and barbarous" stocks would inevitably be extinguished in competition with Anglo-Saxons. No Christian benevolence could check the extinction of lower races, which was decreed by the laws of population. The Irish never arrived at colleges or legislatures and never became mechanics or merchants but crowded the "alms-houses, the prisons, and potter's fields."[33] Such a race was doomed to destruction by the divine laws of population. Similarly, the Negroes, who were "animals" rather than human beings, were certain to be annihilated by their own incompetence once they were freed.[34]

Bushnell made no attempt to reach the Catholics of Hartford, though he fervently supported the Protestant Alliance, which he expected to "revolutionize the Papacy." He gloried in the vastness of its purposes. "We must carry the war into Africa. A great object inspires. The Papacy is weaker at Rome and more vulnerable than at Cincinnati."[35]

Within the city itself, the first concern of the Protestant ministry was to bring the Gospel to the middle and upper classes. The families who controlled the banks and benevolent societies also headed church committees, acted as deacons, and made the major financial contributions to the Congregational and Episcopal churches. Arriving at Hartford's First Church in 1817, Joel Hawes was overwhelmed by "the splendor, the noise, and the trials of a city congregation." Four out of five deacons were not church members, and the brief creed appalled him by its Arminianism. Inflexibly orthodox, he saw his duty clearly. Yet, faced with an urbane, polite society, he had to force himself to "act the minister"; later, fearing he had overdone it, he accused himself of undue severity in his "manner of rebuking sin." After two years he still nervously wondered whether these "fine folk and fastidious lawyers" would be offended by the "barbed arrows" he was obliged to hurl at them. Even the intrepid Charles Grandison Finney, aiding in some of Hawes's revivals, agreed it was impossible among these "fas-

41

tidious and precise" people to call on sinners to "give themselves publicly to God."[36]

There was always the danger that the "fastidious" might
turn to the Episcopal church, where they were not obliged
to abase themselves. Mrs. Sigourney, who became an Episcopalian after her marriage, suggested the appeal of the
church for the refined sensibility. She was delighted with
her new form of worship, "so impressive was the solemnity
of its liturgy, the hallowed beauty of its ordinances." Indignant Congregationalists traced the fateful appeal of Episcopalianism for the wealthy to its social prestige and its indulgence of fashionable vices and extravagances. "To be an
Episcopalian," the *New Englander* dolefully explained, is
"respectable . . . very respectable . . . , and it introduces one
into good society."[37]

Arriving in Hartford in 1831, the Reverend Robbins was
struck by the vehemence of the "Episcopalian controversy."[38] Loyal Congregationalists faced a disheartening
situation. As the Episcopalians increased, families like the
Morgans, the Sigourneys, the Imlays, and the Huntingtons
heightened the splendor, wealth, and appeal of the denomi-
nation. When a new church was needed, St. John's Parish,
with a recessed chancel and pointed windows, purple velvet
trimming on the pulpit, and a white marble fount, was designed especially for the young and wealthy of "churchly
instincts."[39]

Episcopalianism did not require "barbed arrows" or violent conversions. In Hartford strict Congregationalists could
recall the Bishop's agitation for a theater; they knew that the
one rector who indulged in "personal, plain speaking" remained less than a year in Christ Church.[40]

But in spite of the ominous strength of Episcopalianism,
Hawes set about restoring orthodoxy and converting his
congregation. The degree of his revivalistic success is an

42

index to the tensions concealed beneath the urbane decorum of the fastidious. By 1822, church members subscribed to a lengthy creed, and a church "prudential committee" supervised the morals and faith of the congregation. Hawes "preached down" the annual Assembly Balls and aimed his "arrows" so astutely that he could boast ten revivals with over one thousand converts during his ministry.[41]

Nonetheless, Hawes's severity exacted its toll. In 1824 ninety-seven members left his church to form the North Congregational Church; some were Hartford's most prominent citizens. Dedicating the new church for his departing parishioners, Hawes sorrowfully noted the growth of a "taste . . . for a superficial and shewy kind of preaching" in the larger towns of America and warned his former charges against the "kinds of preaching . . . that regales the fancy and the taste, rather than searches the heart and conscience—that deals in pretty thoughts and fine sayings, rather than in the doctrines that are unto salvation."[42] In the face of this austere counsel, the church first called to the pastorate a melancholy minister-poet, Carlos Wilcox. Though pleased with his "spirited and . . . prosperous" congregation, Wilcox struggled vainly for a revival and left the church after a year, on grounds of ill-health.[43] Hawes, analyzing Wilcox' service after his death, wondered whether the poet's "rhetoric" had not diminished his effectiveness but darkly noted that a "class of minds" existed which found such "elegance" appealing.[44]

The church next called Taylorite Samuel Spring, who published a sermon on temperance, exacerbated Tylerites, and four years after his installation departed for an East Hartford church, leaving the congregation bitterly divided over the merits of Taylorite divinity. Horace Bushnell was the church's third minister. By the time of his arrival the church had established a prudential committee, had con-

demned all traffic in "Ardent Spirits," and, according to fac-
tion, waited for rigorous orthodoxy or the excitement of
Taylor's New Divinity.[45]

Bushnell passed his adult life in Hartford; the North
Church was his only pastorate. His situation, like Hawes's,
was not easy at first. A disquieting impression prevailed that
city congregations did not take to country-style sermons.
To fortify, warn, and counsel a vulnerable clergy, Samuel
Miller had published a sermon on "The Difficulties and
Temptations Which Attend the Preaching of the Gospel in
Great Cities."[46] Rejected by a New York church, Joseph
Bellamy decided he was not "polite enough for them" but
was considered suitable only for a backwoods ministry.[47]
The most introspective passages in Bushnell's journals abroad
turned on his social failures. Wounded by the patent reluc-
tance of English divines to let him preach—"Never," he
wrote, "have I suffered more in feeling"—he finally attributed the snubs to his lack of reputation and his unimpressive
conversation.[48]

In Hartford the awkward country boy identified himself
with the city's best society, hesitating to stand apart, the
uncouth, rough, and inacceptable judge of these well-meaning, prosperous citizens whose generosity supported the ref-
ormation of the world. As Bushnell framed his ideal of the
minister, the qualities which eased "personal acceptableness"
focused his ambition. "Conciliation, drawing, leading," not
rude fury, marked gentlemanly persuasion. He wished that
the American minister possessed a "nicer sense of character,"
"moderating austerity, softening hardness, making the unworldly spirit amiable."[49]

The oversights, the complacencies, and the aspirations of
Bushnell's congregation defined his social perspective. Their
perplexities helped frame his questions; their resistances
helped decide his accommodations. Anxious to reach his

44

hearers, anxious for success as he groped to find his full message, he was conciliatory.

The ethos of the business community shaped his way of thinking. In spite of his rural past, he often used the imagery of finance and business. He described God's final profit calculation in His dealings with humanity; the "conquest of grace" seemed like gaining a good credit position. God's free gift of salvation and the destitution of the elect without His mercy figured difficultly within an imagery drawn from rationalized capitalism. God's confidence in the humanity in which He had invested was rational rather than "visionary"; it was that "of a banker whose fund is in." Bushnell encouraged a well-secured and enterprising Christian hope. "As certainly . . . as you succeed, you can be saved."[50]

The rationality of the universe guaranteed that success would follow virtue. If, as Max Weber has argued, early Calvinists assiduously sought wealth in order to possess the "visible signs" of a salvation they endlessly doubted, Bushnell's gospel comfortably relaxed such tensions. His parishioners could go about their business in the tranquil certainty that, by divine ordinance, virtue created riches. God tempted men to industry by lavish rewards and benevolently assured the conjunction of virtue and prosperity. Virtue repressed "vice and extravagance" and tamed "reckless impulses"; it was the source of "patience, frugality, temperance and economy." Thus, the moral man could hardly be poor. Wealth was an index to virtue, "a reward and honor which God delights to bestow upon an upright people."[51]

By more mysterious decree, the relationship worked inversely. Prosperity caused virtue and religion to thrive. A minister could not hope to strengthen religion among an impoverished people, for no one "demoralized by long defeat" was likely to experience a spiritual victory. Poverty brought moral ruin. Christianity could endure only within the closed

45

circuit of respectability and success. "Give me, then, as a minister of God's truth, a money-loving, prosperous and diligent hearer."[52]

The Puritan merchant had been expected to pursue his calling, bound by an ordinate social code of justice, forgoing speculation, accepting success or calamity as providential judgments. But the trade of Bushnell's vision was unreliable; the merchant's purchases were often a "very blind problem"; his risks depended "on things exceedingly occult." Wresting success from fate, he would have reason to exult in his own power. In failure he should not weakly search for the sins which God had condemned but should remember that "nothing but the most unmanly caution" could have kept him safe. The periodic crises of trade were not divine chastisements but part of the cycle of legitimate commerce. While other ministers in times of panic hurled jeremiads against gambling and greed, Bushnell protested that the very nature of credit forced speculations beyond the limits of safety.[53]

Religion, he taught, should not intrude upon business. The law of self-interest prohibited charity in trade; commerce was properly conducted by strict accounting. During the hours of business, merchants were to act "under the laws of trade," reserving "their charities—all their sympathies, allowances, mitigations, merciful accommodations—for a separate chapter of life." Repeatedly, Bushnell called upon the metaphor of flight to convey the religious life to his congregation. The Sabbath served less as a critique of all experience than as an escape from the usual "low torments" of the mind into a temporary freedom, where the soul might "ascend to things congenial to its higher affinities."[54]

An image of the congregation emerges from the sermons —fastidious, wary of religious extravagance, consciously proper, impatient of the claims of the church. "Moral, honorable, . . . beneficent and habitually reverent," they found it difficult to believe that a drastic change of heart was necessary for salvation. The doctrine of total depravity struck them as "unjust and extravagant" and glaringly inappropriate to their experience. Many had a "pride against" salvation by grace; others found the intense "conviction of sin" of New Testament saints contemptible. The Scriptures often offended them by coarseness, and Christ's sacrifice seemed superfluous. Almost all of them suspected religion of imposing ignominious requirements upon the believer.[55]

Bushnell addressed himself to the preferences of his confident, prosperous, and ambitious congregation. He accepted as the "game of life" the race to surpass others in wealth, display, or fame. Though the early Puritans had counseled humility before God's Providence, Bushnell traced the "zest of life" to hazarding and triumphing over the unknown. Repeatedly, he assured his hearers that religion did not require the humiliation of the soul but freed all its powers. The Christian was called to a "large place and . . . great victories." "You will never be driven into God's kingdom to be sheltered there from the loss and ignominy of a defeated life. Salvation is success and nothing else."[56]

But Bushnell was not always content to rationalize the ways of his congregation. His past and his vocation isolated him, and with rough directness he occasionally accused his people of moral failure. Measuring the disparity between the early Christians and his own society, he indicted America's middle class with the sudden violence of despair. "Probably there was never any class of Christians in the world . . . so little penetrated by Christian love." Though his congregation had size, power, intelligence, it failed to reveal the spirit of Christ. "You have the power of contributors and patrons, but not of witnesses."[57]

Once he preached on "Respectable Sin," struggling to give

47

significance to guilt and sin for a people who lived with conscious probity. "The sin is here, and the sin that wants salvation; but it is sin so thoroughly respectable as to make it very nearly impossible to produce any just impression of its deformity." Bushnell's message was even more stifled because he did not, like the later Social Gospellers, make poverty and misery the index of middle-class guilt. He chose instead to define sin apart from social problems, in the sole extremity of man's relationship with God. "What can you know of sin, . . . when you are living so respectably and maintain, in the outward life, a show of so great integrity?"

To his complacent, industrious, well-meaning people Bushnell counseled self-doubt, humility, terror. There was no peace for the upright; the most dutiful of men might be radically corrupt; the most seemly might be obnoxious to God. Bushnell himself faltered in his understanding of this strange form of sin; the sermon was without precedent or successor; the accusation was vague. Yet he spoke from the conviction that "if all the inward shapes" of his hearers' lives were known, many of the most respected might prove as depraved as the city's outcasts.[58]

Bushnell continued to trumpet the alliance of virtue and success. Nonetheless, rejection lurked in the recesses of his most genial conciliations, and his rhetoric on behalf of power stretched over sharp mistrust. The happy conviction that militant goodness always triumphed in the struggle for survival quickly paled when that struggle threatened to widen.

In his feverish opposition to woman suffrage, Bushnell betrayed many fears. "Let us have a place of quiet, and some quiet minds which the din of our public war never embroils. Let a little of the sweetness and purity, and . . . of the simple religion of life remain." If women traded their unworldly sanctity for worldly victories, they would inevitably be corrupted, for power "naturally runs to oppression." Only marriage saved love from extinction; only women, outside worldly frays, could exalt existence by their charity and their closeness to God. Once women took part in the warfare of business or politics, the womanly, last symbol of God's Gospel, would be destroyed.[59]

As Bushnell's experience gradually turned his imagination to the figure of Christ, he found a judgment on the world. In the midst of Hartford propriety he pondered on the image of Christ with such lonely and narrow scrutiny that he wondered whether he himself, confronted with a man so alien, odd, and exiled, would not turn away. Eternally separate from the world, Christ was not a popular Savior. "Christ did not wrest victories from fate by the energy of His will, but by a loving, passive submission." Meek, disreputable, scorning propriety, the figure and message of Christ aligned at no point with the successful merchant. No one could discern the Gospel but the "meek and humble." Who, then, were the world's Christians? Those whom the laws of population had doomed to extinction, the outcast, the animal—the Negroes were now "the true Nazarenes and Galileans of the world."[60]

In such tensions of value Bushnell held his faith. If he predicted that the Negroes would build the new Jerusalem, he insisted that this holy kingdom could not be in America. He was committed to the middle-class society of America which controlled his future and which saw in success the justification of privilege and complacency. Within Hartford, Bushnell quickly identified himself with his "worldly, money-loving, prosperous, but strenuous" congregation and, like his congregation, ignored the numerous poor who had "failed" within America's competitive society. Unlike later

Social Gospelers, Bushnell had no compensating ideal of a wealthy paternalism that might guide, protect, and redeem the poor. Neither the city's economy nor its ethos of individualistic enterprise bent to the conception of such an integrated order.

Yet the Negroes and the Catholics, left on the outskirts of the city's charity, remained to plague the conscience by the stubborn grimness of their lives. For Bushnell these dark, rejected figures became at times symbols of a pervasive desertion that included his congregation and even himself. Yet, at other times, their wretchedness served only to set off the bright and fitting rule of Anglo-Saxon energy.

That the sermon was the unit of Bushnell's presentation made his inconsistency less perceptible. But the conflict was crucial. Questions Bushnell could not completely avoid stood ready to destroy the pattern which merged Christianity and success. He did not think in terms of the Puritan injunction to be in, yet not of, the world. His imagination was straitened by the dualism of power and failure. One mode of life, he felt, must closely answer the Christian command; one must be the Anti-Christ. If the choice had to be between corrupting power or passive failure, however, he himself hesitated. The alternatives somehow corresponded to the tensions of his experience. In all the haste of his eagerness to make his way, he was to be repeatedly entangled by a Gospel he could not ignore—an uncompromising Gospel, uncongenial to his people and his success.

One day he baldly announced to his congregation that the judgments of eternity would capsize the moral decisions of the world. Yet where Melville, viewing the same disjunction between the secular and divine law in *Billy Budd*, saw in it an archetype of the Crucifixion, Bushnell merely rejoiced that the divine record would allow the world to proceed on its decorous if mistaken way until Judgment

Day.[61] Christianity was not so blurred for him as to have lost all form; like Nietzsche and Kierkegaard, he saw its alien commands. But whether contempt for the weak or the dream of the City of God was more compelling remained indeterminate. Disdain and allegiance played against each other in his faith.

V. The Security of Christian Nurture

Life was abundant and disturbing for Bushnell during his thirties. He and his bride took possession of their own home; soon, two daughters and a son brought them new responsibilities, hope, and love. His vocation itself proved exacting. One of the city's most wealthy and prominent men, a deacon in his church, complained about him to everyone who would listen. Bushnell heard of grumblings and unfounded accusations. Conscious that he had "only a slight hold" on his people, he feared he would be dismissed.[1]

The early years of an American Congregationalist pastor had become a probationary period, during which, everyone knew, a "very few" influential parishioners could easily bring about the minister's dismissal. To escape the lonely hegira from church to smaller church, the minister had to please congregations that were frequently divided and increasingly critical. Religious periodicals urgently directed him to the successful methods of public persuasion, pressing upon him the models of senators and lawyers who met the problem with enviable éclat.[2]

Contentions which split congregations, ministers, and divinity schools into hostile camps made the minister's position even more uneasy. He could have little hope of settling tranquilly into fixed theological conventions. Some members of the congregation militantly battled over a series of crucial issues, while others were bored with the whole agitation.

Among people trained by decades of controversy, the minister could not hope to obscure his position with irenic vagueness. The questions were too clear. He knew that colleagues, congregation, and townspeople would be looking for the statements which would define his stance, secure his friends, and alert his enemies.

Bushnell soon discovered that a new minister had to chalk and follow a tortuous line. Not long after his settlement, he discovered that an East Windsor professor was widely denouncing his heresies.[3] Bushnell's church was fighting over the "New Haven controversy," and within the parish, as a recent Yale graduate, he was bound to be suspected by anti-Taylorites. The possibility of a shrunken congregation loomed darkly before him; other Hartford churches stood ready to welcome malcontents of every persuasion. There was Hawes's church ushering in scores of the regenerate with every new revival; there was the Episcopalian Christ Church deploring revivalistic crudeness and decorously increasing in size, wealth, and prestige.

The theological vigilance of Hartford was exercised in a small compass. Solicitude centered on time-worn New England controversies—the role of the will in regeneration, the violence of the "new birth," the use of "new measures" in revivals. Bushnell's first book (*Views of Christian Nurture*) grew from these local anxieties. Success had to begin at home, in the strengthening of his own church against defections and schisms.

Yet the young minister who hoped for a larger audience and a wider fame encountered further dilemmas. He had to find a message which would arrest a nation barraged by sermons, speeches, newspapers, periodicals, and books. Assured in advance that theology bored practical and informed democrats, he had yet to discover a subject on which he could speak with authority. If he could not afford to antagonize his people or his colleagues, neither could he ignore the interests of the larger American public. Though the public read voraciously, it read only what it pleased. If the people's insistent demands for information, romance, and sentimental plaints of poetry revealed some general craving, the minister could not meet their necessities by a discourse on human agency. He had instead to discern and assuage the central sickness of the society.

Already thirty-one when he started his life work, Bushnell had for many years felt the burden and the promise of personal power. But the first decade of his pastorate passed in the frustration of incomplete achievements and partial recognitions. He was fumbling, often discouraged; once a robust farmer, he endured poor health. Though he railed sardonically at his enemies, he did not dissipate all his energy in spleen. He was used to hard work, and he stubbornly applied himself to the task of winning his congregation's loyalty by the promise of a successful ministry.

By Bushnell's time, one way of deciding ministerial success was well established. "The fruits of the minister's labors," or the number of his conversions, offered a clear, objective test of his efficacy. Revival statistics adorned commemorative discourses on ministers and crowded the pages of the *Religious Intelligencer* and the *Connecticut Evangelical Magazine*. In Taylor's and Beecher's crusade against Unitarianism and religious apathy, revivals had been decisive; everyone agreed that New England had been "singularly blessed" in such outpourings of God's grace.

"Better be ignorant, unskilled anywhere else than here," Enoch Pond warned in *The Young Pastor's Guide*. Revivals thoroughly tested the minister, revealing his ability to "get at people," and his hold of that touchstone of wisdom, common sense. So certain was the test that for Charles Finney it made Christ's preaching "success" uncertain, though Finney finally decided Jesus had done quite well "considering the circumstances under which he labored."[4]

In Hartford, Bushnell dutifully entered the lists to try his skill at winning souls. During the first year of his ministry, Bushnell ardently urged the perpetual readiness of the Holy Spirit to aid the soul anxious for regeneration. With particular fervor he addressed those who put off "beginning . . . the Christian life" from fear of failure. In the second year of his pastorate, when Hawes was converting many of the wealthier members of the First Church, Bushnell assailed his people with their duty to struggle for God as Jacob had done, quieting Old School fears by the assurance that such struggle was compatible with "the most absolute notion of dependence." He ended the sermon with a pressing anticipation. "What is wanting in us is that we be able to follow on. . . . The little cloud is even now visible. In that sign . . . our faith may behold abundance of rain and that to come speedily." Yet no revival followed. In 1834, forty-one came in by profession of faith; in 1835, only four; and in 1836, twelve.[5]

Measured by the accepted standards, the new minister seemed a failure, and he had not yet forged clear standards of his own. In 1836, discouraged, he was tempted to return to the detested job of schoolteaching. In 1836 he published an article on "The Spiritual Economy of Revivals of Religion," hoping to destroy the "despair and lethargy" which accompanied the identification of religion and revivals. He had found the "most disheartening impediment to the Christian minister" in the widespread conviction that religion depended only on revivals.[6]

Throughout Bushnell's career, revivals challenged his competence, for he never succeeded in inducing large-scale "seasons of refreshment." When he prepared an assessment of his ministry after twenty years' service, he faced the thin statistics of his church's increase, and the customary flow of words suddenly bogged down in false starts. Was the test of the usefulness of his ministry, as he wrote and then crossed out, measured by the "fruits gathered?"[7] It is uncertain whether he ever finally decided; clearly failure threatened. In the late eighteen-thirties, with no other achievement to relieve his doubt, with an unsatisfied and watchful congregation, failure must have frequently seemed inevitable.

Yet in his attempts to start a revival Bushnell must have perceived the dangers, even of success. "The business, the bustle, the dissipation, the etiquette" of cities somehow rebuffed revivals; Bushnell's own congregation was largely dominated by men who had left the church of the revivalist Hawes. Religious "deadness" reliably followed religious ecstasy, and the minister was usually blamed for the decline. Meanwhile, medical authorities and Unitarians were warning a health-pursuing public of the baleful effects of excessive religious excitement.[8]

To avoid offending the fastidious, the minister had to be circumspect. Many of the orthodox deplored the frequent use of "new measures" by "low-bred men" and lamented the "coarseness" and lack of "refinement" in Finney's style.[9] A vocabulary of protest against revivals was gaining currency, backed by the religions which were attracting New England's upper classes away from Congregationalism. It dwelt on such terms as "gentle," "tender," "delicate," in describing the proper ecstasy of the soul. In New York and Connecticut the Episcopalians criticized the drabness of revivalistic religion, its sacrifice of social amenities, its neglect of baptism, the church, and the family.

During the eighteen-thirties Connecticut Episcopalianism became increasingly High Church. In 1843 Hartford's St. John's Church published a parishioner's brochure on "Eliza, the Child that Grew in Grace," and Bishop Brownell's charge to the clergy enumerated the "Errors of the Times," which turned out to be the frantic quest for a "new birth," the neglect of Christian baptism and nurture, and the alternating enthusiasm and apathy of New England Congregationalism.[10]

Even sympathizers of revivals were occasionally checked by the indiscriminate statistical avidity of revivalists. In Hartford Finney and Nettleton had campaigned vigorously among the destitute, but the church they founded for the poor, once left to its own and Hartford's devices, soon settled into middle-class membership.[11] Hartford's "better" classes had aims and anxieties that diverted them from the sustained conversion or companionship of the poor.

Bushnell himself, certain that the "inferior stocks" were perishing, was not tempted to populate his church with the races of the doomed. The ideal church of his vision was to act upon the community by its testifying presence, not by mere "will-work." The laws of population would insure its final dominion without revivals. This dream of a Christian community—in which love and the health of the Anglo-Saxon stock together overpowered the ignoble—increasingly possessed his imagination. In this question as in others, Bushnell's interest followed the lines of middle-class concerns.

Hartford families had more intimate worries than the conversion of their poorer neighbors. Their own children threatened to become strangers to their way of life. The dissipation of the sons of some eminent citizens crept into the city's records. Whittier, invited to join a club of prominent young men, refused after his shocked discovery of their immorality.[12] In 1834, following Hawes's revival, prominent citizens briefly attempted to reform the frivolities of Hartford's youth, and a young woman converted by Finney valiantly tried to save a "class of young men," both eminent and wealthy, who had "fallen into bad habits and . . . moral decay."[13]

Throughout the Northeast in the nineteenth century, families suffered anxieties like Hartford's. As cities multiplied at the expense of the country, parents fearfully watched their sons depart for the "many . . . temptations" of the city. Beyond the reach of rural society and parental sanctions, these young men, living in boarding houses, acting as clerks, and dreaming of wealth, seemed dangerously emancipated to people used to a firmer family structure. The city's lures, as catalogued by James Alexander, included "the night cellar, the low concert, the ball, the equivocal show, . . . the billiard-room, and the den of infamy. . . ." In the *Christian Spectator*, a correspondent bleakly divulged that of his many acquaintances who had gone to New York not one had become a Christian "or even a Sabbath-School teacher." Instead, they had "cast off the . . . fear of sin" that they had learned in childhood.[14]

This social mobility, which unsettled the most intimate relationships men and women knew, created a painful need for reassurances. The fiction of gift books repeated tales of wicked young men in the city but frequently ended on a note of salvation. "A Profligate's Regard for His Mother" described the accepted mode of redemption. "How often has the profligate son, in the very midst of his dissipation and sin, been led to reflect and repent by a recollection of a mother's prayers and tears!"[15]

The bastion of the home was set against the disintegration suffered by mobile sons amid city temptations. The home was the symbol of religion, of simplicity, and of permanence; and the early associations which clustered around it formed a permanent reserve of moral strength. Poems and stories on the redemptive power of early piety crowded the pages of the *Sabbath School Treasury* and the *Congrega-*

tional Visitor and inspired best-selling novels, gift books, and poems. In the home, hidden from the "passion-stirring and tumultuous scenes of life," the divinely meek nature of women redeemed fallen husbands and sons "reeling from the haunts of dissipation."[16] "Let the wayward son stop in his profanities and remember a dying mother's counsel," commanded Bushnell in a sermon on "The Heavenly State."

As young men left home for the hazardous promise of urban success, parents through the Northeast were bewildered, anxious, and proud. Out of their emotional duress came a new image of religious experience. As religion was a cherished part of the imperiled past, so the new pattern retained the familiar terms of theology. Popular literature divided experience into a dualism of good and evil, of salvation and reprobation, of innocence and corruption. Yet these very similarities manifested and implemented a revolution in general religious beliefs.

Calvinism taught the depravity of all men and God's gracious election of some to salvation. Evil at birth, no one could attain perfection; still, men were to serve God diligently in their callings while spiritually they remained dead to the world. But the literature eagerly read by nineteenth-century Americans ordered experience differently. The world that "tainted" and "defiled" was contrasted with the home, where purity reigned. A pervasive suspicion of the changing society nourished the dream of a cloistered, pristine innocence. The *Friendship Offering* decided that angels must weep to see the soul "all pure and brilliant" descend to the earth—"that huge shadow of woe and crime—through which no winged thing . . . can penetrate unstained." Moved at the spectacle of infants so pure and doomed, the *Rose of Sharon* tenderly requested speedy deaths for the young.[17]

The projected purity of childhood stretched a white backdrop that set the world's depravity in stark relief. The literary convention provided the vehicle for jeremiads that enthusiastic democrats, buoyed up in the high tide of progress, might otherwise have repelled. "Which is worst and farthest from God," demanded Bushnell, "these innocent exuberances of life, or the covetous, overcaring, overworking, enviously plotting, sobriety of their parents?"[18]

Thus the mother, exempt like the child from competitive struggles, provided the key to salvation. Yet if mothers were convinced by the ubiquitous assertions of their power, they did not know how to exploit it. References to the failures of family government, to family tragedies, and to the wanton eagerness of young people to leave home suggest that their doubts were founded in familial instabilities.[19] Some felt failure of tradition made women seek out authoritative counsel, the latest information, the reassurance of mutual confession in "maternal societies." Advisory novels and periodicals multiplied and sold. Mrs. Sigourney, Catherine Sedgwick, and Sarah Hale dropped fiction and poetry for domestic counseling, and in 1839 the *Ladies' Repository* quitted the "haunts of romance" to concentrate upon woman's "social ministry to the human heart."[20] Perplexed and hopeful, women were emotionally sustained by the assurance that their training could triumph over the temptations of the world.

There were no professional psychologists to guide them, but the clergy leaped in to remove the breach between the generations. Trained in mental philosophy, guardians of the moral order, the ministry could link the present to the familiar past. Faced by the hazy outlines of their children's future lives, parents clutched at religion with an avidity they failed to muster for themselves alone. Out of its new needs, the American reading public created a new role for the clergy.

In his first book in 1846 Bushnell addressed this public,

counseling parents on the proper methods of Christian nurture. Like other Americans, he based his child psychology on the Scottish philosophy. American ministers, authors, and educationalists had long discoursed on the waxlike infant mind on which sensations and emotions could be indelibly impressed and indissolubly joined. So susceptible a creature should be easily molded. Imitative and ductile, the child could be led where the parents willed during the decisive early years when the character was being set.

Religious leaders customarily deplored the wasted years of childhood, in which religious impressions might have been permanently and preservingly engraven on the mind. For it was common knowledge by the nineteenth century that parents were not training their children in religion. Several decades of pleas for the restitution of family religion testified to a continuing neglect. In the nineteenth century the General Association of Connecticut recalled parents to their duties while ministers in New London, Fairfield, and Hartford bewailed the ominous decline in family religion. Periodicals and sermons kept up the cry; Presbyterian ministers and the *Princeton Review* vainly reprimanded those whose neglect caused a decrease in baptisms.[21] Yet parents proved intransigent. With a grim prophecy of the imminent ruin of the church, Joel Hawes surrendered to parental objections against teaching the catechism to children.[22]

In their concern for family religion, orthodox ministers prepared the way for the sentimental heresies of the 1830's and 1840's. But if ministers stressed the importance of the child, in the early nineteenth century they continued to preach that regeneration required a drastic transformation. Such a decisive change consorted oddly with the yielding plasticity of the child's nature, but in the early decades of the century the triumphs of revivalism and republican individualism obscured the implications of the accepted associationalist psychology. Since the late eighteenth century, widespread revivals had reaffirmed the Puritan expectation that saints could be distinguished, while disciples of Jonathan Edwards shared his conviction that divine election would be marked by clear and distinct signs. Throughout New England such ministers resolved to end the Half-Way Covenant: fighting congregations, losing their pastorates, witnessing the division of their churches, they were finally victorious.[23]

Revivalistic theology was aided by the fact that the Revolutionary and post-Revolutionary generations denied the right of the past to control the present and believed that no individual's fate could be indentured to another's. The individualism which had made it impossible for Emmons, Bellamy, and Hopkins to accept imputed guilt or righteousness, made the decisive experience of the individual seem essential to salvation. Nathanael Emmons was characteristic of his time when he announced that the church was a "voluntary society, formed by a voluntary compact" and that God could not enter a covenant with man without his deliberate, adult consent.[24]

In spite of republican and revivalistic individualism, however, the picture of the "innocent" child made an increasing and fateful appeal to the ministry. In many ways the child was becoming a center of hope. The American Sunday School Union was struck by the resistance of prominent adults to clerical criticism and by the felicitous, contrasting docility of children under reproof.[25] If adult obstinacy plagued the minister, preaching to children could easily bypass the "rough hills of obstruction," as Bushnell pointed out.[26]

The necessity of suiting doctrine to children facilitated a genial reconstruction of theology. For childish apprehension, doctrine had to be set in an "appealing form," little geared to the "offence of the cross." Religion was speedily linked with the innocence, love, and simplicity of which the child was symbol; language adjusted to a child's understanding could express "the conceptions of an angel," according to the American Sunday School Union. Such simplifications proved generally enticing. Soon the Union could jubilantly report that parents and neighbors, who rejected "more elaborate" religious works, were enjoying Sunday School books.[27]

As ministers set out to meet the needs of the child, religious experience was redefined. The popular *Letters of Pestalozzi on the Education of Infancy* announced that the infant heart could be led only by love. Given the child's responsive goodness, religious anguish was unnecessary. Books stressed that the child was injured by the violence of "premature excitement," and the best-selling *Mother at Home* urged that no terror or crisis was needed, for the child's conversions could take place imperceptibly, leaving no memory of the precise moment of regeneration.[28]

The divine nature was also delineated to suit the child's preferences. A God of wrath and judgment could not "appeal," and God was increasingly presented through the image of the Lamb. If the adult were to recall religion with pleasure, nothing gloomy should be associated with it in childhood, and authors amiably concluded that the smiling aspects of religion best met the case. As all emotions were rooted in perceptions, the child's feeling for his mother began and determined his eventual love for God. "How easy it is," marveled Mrs. Sedgwick in *Home*, "to interweave the religious with the domestic affections."[29]

According to orthodox New England Calvinism, children were depraved, and regeneration came in a shattering choice with which the individual began a new life. According to the accepted psychology, the child was a pliant entity whose eventual decisions were governed by early associations. Given the orthodox rationale, the minister should logically have concentrated upon the adult congregation. Yet he had found middle-class adults prone to criticism, pride, and religious apathy, while the business world, which engrossed their interests, seemed hostile to the traditions in which piety and the "fireside" had flourished together. Only in concern for the education of the young did the interests of religion and the middle-class adult population meet without friction. Out of the conflict of dogma and situation came the opportunity for a new reading of theology.

Open discontent with revivalism appeared first in the German Reformed and Presbyterian churches. In 1843 John Nevin, professor in the German Reformed Mercersburg Seminary, published *The Anxious Bench*, attacking the "new measures" by which Finney and Taylor had quickened the pace of repentance. Trained in the idealism of Hegel and Schleiermacher, Nevin proposed to replace the individualism of the New Divinity by recognition of the organic nature of society and the church. Taylor's doctrines, it was said, substituted jerky excitements for the growth of God's spirit in the soul and underestimated the ingrown evil in the world and humanity. To offset the sin "rooted in the race," the individual should be nourished from childhood in the true church. Held within the "kingdom of grace," the child would grow gently into a Christian life, without the agony of a spiritual transformation.[30]

In a vein more native than Nevin's, the Presbyterian church formulated an extensive critique of revivalistic New Divinity, which under cover of the Plan of Union was infiltrating Presbyterianism. Led by Charles Hodge at Princeton, Presbyterians reaffirmed the doctrine of the Abrahamic covenant, promising that God would recognize and receive the baptized child if he remained "faithful to his baptismal vows." God would probably impute Christ's righteousness to the baptized child; in any case the child, like the adult church member, was presumptively one of the elect. Since only God knew the members of the true, invisible church, the visible church was composed of saints and sinners.[31]

Ignoring contemporary psychology and neglecting parental anxieties, the Presbyterian and German Reformed doctrines met none of the time's insistent queries as to education and gave no promises that could vie with the relief of a revival's conversions. Nor could the Abrahamic covenant be adapted to popular fictional or poetic conventions. Congregational ministers and the more popular writers passed by the churchly theories of Nevin and Hodge. They focused instead upon the "Mother at Home," finding here the promise of redemption.

The resultant literature of the Sunday School Union and of the religious annuals often subverted orthodoxy, but in so sanctioned and fragmentary a way that even conservative Congregationalists did not sound an alarm. The prolonged war against theology had created an indifference in which confusion bred. Though neither gift-book language nor gift-book sensibility could be held within the categories of Christian orthodoxy, no one pointed out the conflict; and in spite of the concern for education, ministers were still tested by revival statistics. It was left to an obscure Hartford minister to integrate the commitments of the time within Protestant theology.

Bushnell met the contradictory values of his audience: the individualism that promoted revivals, the gentility that feared them, the troubled parents who neglected religion and worried about the irreligion of their children, the orthodoxy that fostered the Sunday School and insisted on man's radical corruption. He saw and testified to the desperate peril of the church. The vein had "run out"; the American churches were "exhausted." In 1834 and 1835 the North Church had no infant baptisms; from 1835 to 1838, only thirty-seven. In 1838 the church resolved that baptism had been "too lightly held by this church in years past" and voted that the pastor should give a series of talks on the meaning of the sacrament. Yet the issue remained delicate; Bushnell's talks antagonized Deacon Terry, who complained that the child should be taught that he "was all the time . . . rebelling, and that he must yield himself to God as a living sacrifice." In 1845 church officer James Hosmer joined Hawes's First Church and in 1846, with three other Hartford laymen, endowed an East Windsor professorship in honor of the revivalist Ashahel Nettleton.[32]

Nonetheless, the new minister continued. He used Scottish epistemology, the language of sentiment, and the idealization of childhood to undermine Episcopalian and Unitarian critiques of revivalistic Congregationalism. To an anxious middle class he promised that with a proper Christian nurture no child need be lost. If he daringly rejected contemporary individualism, he instructed his audience in the means of salvation. Under his hand the materials of contemporary thought were shaped into a vision of Christian community.

The work began with the requested talks and with articles published in the *Christian Spectator* and the *New Englander.* Bushnell was fighting on several fronts. In the *New Englander* he lambasted Bishop Brownell with ponderous sarcasm, accusing Episcopalianism of pandering to the "folly" of the "thoughtless and gay." The frenzied, heavy-handed attack was a characteristic explosion of Bushnell's insecurity and was, characteristically, followed by doctrinal reconciliation. Later the same year, he published "The Kingdom of Heaven as a Grain of Mustard Seed," which urged that Christian growth replace revivalistic convulsions.[33]

A trip to the Continent for his health intervened between

the articles and the eventual book on Christian nurture. In England Bushnell painfully discovered his own obscurity,[34] and upon his return he agreed to incorporate the articles in a book to be published by the Massachusetts Sunday School Society. Faced with the finished work, the Sunday School Committee hesitated, weighed possible reactions, required changes, and published *Views of Christian Nurture* finally in 1846. But the definition of orthodoxy had become so shaky that after an attack from the East Windsor Theological Seminary on the book's heresies, the committee hastily suppressed it.

Views of Christian Nurture was based upon the empiricism and associationalism of Scottish philosophy. The projected infant mirrored the familiar image of gift annuals—delicate, tender, close to innocence. Like Taylor, Bushnell insisted that the baby was amoral rather than depraved; "a mere passive lump," he was molded by the surrounding environment. His character was cast by the perceptions that poured in upon his consciousness. The family's tone of life and the atmosphere of the home should be infused with love and piety, for the generations were linked in close dependence, the child being formed before his soul matured.[35]

The parents taught religion not by doctrine but by the reality of the impressions given in their lives. The love of the mother revealed the love of Christ. Parents were given by God "to personate and finite Himself, and gather to such human motherhood and fatherhood, a piety transferable to Himself." Since parents enforced moral laws upon the child, they became for him the "natural and moral image" of God. Knowledge could not reach beyond the child's experience. Bending theory to accommodate the child's nature, parents would avoid the "repulsive" aspects of religion but would teach the discipline and love which together constituted the Christian message. Knowing his family's just

67

rule and its forgiving love, the child would have adequate foundations for Christian faith.[36]

The family could form a unit so touched by Christ that the house would be a citadel for pure religion. Within its walls the child would enter upon religious experience without the agony of despair. He would "open upon the world as one spiritually renewed, not remembering the time when he went through a technical experience, but seeming to have loved what is good from his earliest years."[37]

Not every class could aspire equally to the benefits of Christian nurture. Bushnell suspected that children growing up in a "filthy and loose habit" would be insensitive to corruption. The "dirt upon their persons and clothing" would probably stain their consciences as well. He cautioned against feeding children bonbons and recommended that the child be dressed like a Christian, since a Christian body was unlikely to contain a pagan soul. The rewards of Christian nurture fell to those families whose virtuous health and prosperity insured that they would eventually outpopulate the world.[38]

With grace so knit to circumstances, it was difficult to unravel a crucial apostasy. Bushnell maintained that Christian virtue was achieved only after "a struggle with evil, a fall and a rescue." Yet, analyzed through associationalism, sin and virtue were necessarily defined through family government and familial emotions. Since the child could understand the distinction between right and wrong and could lovingly obey the moral law, Bushnell promised that he could achieve regeneration. Under such a dispensation, in a society which adored the child for his plastic innocence and praised the middle-class home for its gracious affections, the atoning sacrifice of Christ did not seem a prime necessity. The revolt against God and salvation through the sacrifice of God did not easily fit the pattern. The center of *Christian Nurture* was the home.

Yet the book provided a critique as well as a paean of Bushnell's audience. It was not only a book on child care; it aimed to transform the life of Christian adults. If Bushnell could not appeal to his public as Christians, he knew they would listen as parents. Instead of spending their lives in a worldliness interrupted only by spasmodic revivals and facile contributions, parents would understand the far reach of their Christian obligation. Activities had no value unless they came from love; a quality of being, not a series of acts, was required for Christian existence.

A church composed of such Christian families would manifest the spirit of Christ to the world. It would convert not by a "prodigious slaughter among . . . sinners" but by the force of its presence. "Her Christ-like graces of love, purity, truth, and beneficence, are a divine atmosphere about her. . . . To approach her is to be convinced of sin, righteousness, and a judgment to come."[39] Christian nurture culminated in a historic church pervaded by the Holy Spirit. Like Schleiermacher, Bushnell developed the ideal of an organic church, growing within the world, yet set apart from it. Such a church would be continuous testimony to the living spirit of Christ. Its very existence would have converting power on the outer world, while within its saving ordinances its children would graciously grow to Christian adulthood.

In this dream Bushnell returned to the Puritan ideal of a society redeemed by the church, but unlike the semiautonomous Puritan congregations, the church of Bushnell's vision was unified, organic, and of cumulative power. Eventually, he prophesied, such a church would embrace the world, assimilating the insights of all the varied sects in a comprehensive truth. The hope was ecumenical not sectarian; it poised against the individualism of the time the conviction that past and present were necessarily linked and that their union could be holy and redeeming.

In his concern for the church as an organic power, Bushnell stood apart from his age. In the "promiscuous assemblage" of a church congregation, Emerson could find no bonds adequate to justify common prayer, and exalted the lecture hall as the true church of the day. While Bushnell required that the church testify through its felt, inspired presence to the dominion of Christ, Emerson asked of the coming church only that it announce "the algebra and mathematics of ethical law"; while Bushnell required that society use man's inevitable dependence as the means to his redemption, Emerson hoped that the "new church" would send man home to his "central solitude."[40]

Even among the orthodox the ideal of the church had faded. To conservative James Alexander, the church seemed a "casual group of waiting persons." In orthodox churches men read newspapers during prayers, and ladies, before the services began, tapped their feet to polka tunes. By 1866, the *Congregational Quarterly* could easily imagine a "true church" no member of which was a "true Christian." Conservative churchmen were not enthusiastic at Bushnell's picture of a closely linked society. The *Christian Observatory* warned that Bushnell's organic church would undermine personal responsibility by an ennervating collectivism, while the *Christian Review* damned it as "downright socialism."[41]

Reading reviews of his first book, however, the turbulent, ambitious minister, now in his mid-forties, must often have been glad he had published it himself, after the Sunday School Committee's suppression. Only Bennett Tyler, safely cloistered from contemporary pressures in East Windsor Seminary, blasted the book totally. Christianity could never be made attractive to the natural man, Tyler insisted, and the sweet disguises used to lure the child betrayed the Gospel. The soul's corruption was inalienable; no impressions could wean it from its depravity. "Educated by angels, amid the glories of heaven," the child would remain a sinner. In Tyler's legalistic attack, a choked, outraged sense of Christianity struggled for expression through the provincial, timeworn formulas of New England Calvinism.[42]

Periodicals of the Presbyterian, Episcopal, and German Reformed churches praised Bushnell's criticism of the necessity for violent rebirth, his concern with the family, his insight into the organic nature of experience. They remonstrated only against his naturalism. Hodge complained in the *Princeton Review* that Bushnell had left no role to special grace, while the *Episcopalian Review* expostulated that not the family but the church and its sacraments were the vehicle of grace.

Unitarians and liberal Congregationalists saw a harbinger of the millennium in the methods of *Christian Nurture*. The *New Englander* delightedly pointed out that a mother's forgiveness could supplant the need to understand justification by faith and that a mother's glance might convert as well as "the look which Christ gave Peter."[43] A blissful domesticity could supply the essentials of Christian life.

Yet Bushnell was himself discontent with the era of Anglo-Saxon beatitude he foresaw. After all, he had rebelled against Taylor, not on behalf of slumbering infant innocence, but because of "that wonderful power" by which man became a sinner. Like Blake and Shelley, he was attracted by defiance of God. Life derived its meaning, he told his bourgeois congregation, "not by any computation of reason" but by "wild disorders," "the distempers and storms" of passion. It was hard to hold a steady image of the heroic in the setting of Bushnell's life, where the alternatives of sheltered innocence or worldly corruption seemed more

71

evident. But if man was a "demon" who dared "confront the Almighty and tear himself away from his throne," such apostasy could not be remedied by abstinence from bonbons or by tidy clothes. The divine counterpart of the demonic was the wrath of God. As Bushnell saw, redemption required not the childlike appeals of a Jesus but the power of a Christ.[44]

Bushnell's dream of sequestered innocence was thus intermittently crossed by his fear that man was essentially corrupt. His fear saved him from an easy belief in a perfect society; it forced upon him the paradox of Christian redemption. If his seemly public shook his conviction of condemnation, his terror occasionally erupted into warning. God's love was "visibly tempered with dread." Overriding the desires of the human heart, God in his anger demanded payment in pain and torment for every sin.[45]

Such recurrent visions of the Old Testament God kept Bushnell from resting finally with the promise of familial grace. If his sense of human evil hindered his consistency, it also forced him to profounder investigations of human history and Christian redemption. But in 1847 his first long work had ordered many current, scattered faiths within a religious rationale.

VI. The Expedient of Eloquence

By 1848 Bushnell was author of a book that had been heralded, berated, praised, and suppressed. His name had become known; his peculiar mixture of conservatism and liberalism had been recognized and weighed. Yet his achievement seemed to lead nowhere. He could scarcely become a leader in the Sunday School movement, when the Massachusetts Sunday School Society had condemned his book. The other focal concern of *Christian Nurture*, the vision of a church at the center of Christian experience, failed to interest Congregationalists. The stricter Calvinists had pinned their hopes on revivals, while the liberals, busily fighting Episcopalians, shied away from such ecclesiasticism.

Christian Nurture thus solved few personal problems. Bushnell had still to define a role effective enough to satisfy his ambition and his conscience, free enough to accommodate his originality, and catholic enough to meet his temperamental desire and professional need for reconciliation. The task promised to be difficult, set as it had to be within the limits of his vocation and his time.

Bushnell's point of departure was fixed; he entered unpropitiously upon the stage of nineteenth-century America as a Protestant minister. Only an archaic presumption would permit the minister to exact attention on the basis of his calling. Democratic self-confidence was aggressively equalitarian, and the democratic public was besieged by articulate

73

and flattering pleas for its attention. Ministers were everywhere cautioned against professional arrogance, which merely insulted the laity. Diffident before his self-confident audience, Ezra Stiles Gannett announced that he resorted to the pulpit only as a "convenient place of address" and wore his clerical robes to hide his "awkward delivery."[1]

All over the country the pulpit was being lowered by the prevailing cry for equality. Pleased by the trend, the *Religious Magazine* and the *Christian Spectator* pointed out that the minister could now achieve a sympathetic "fervor of feeling" with his audience, from which his lofty isolation had excluded him. As his job was to make the people "feel that the heart of the minister" was with them, the "artificial elevation" of the pulpit along with awesome solemnity and erudition were serious handicaps. For what, after all, demanded the *Christian Examiner*, did the preaching of the pulpit amount to "in a country where people think for themselves," beside the "preaching of the Bible, and . . . of nature, and . . . of common sense"?[2]

At best the minister was one of the people. Though aging ministers of an earlier generation clung to their smallclothes and forbidding mien, the younger clergy shrank from professional peculiarities. Emerson decided that it was the "best part of the man . . . that revolts most against being a minister," and Edwards Park, dismayed by the folios written in "schools, and garrets, and cloisters," called upon divines to compose in the midst of "a more sympathetic and social life."[3] The easy flow, the familiarity, the brevity of the "best conversation" should be the minister's model. He could urge his case effectively while observing the circumspection of a gentleman.

The broken careers and the expressed discontent of prominent ministers revealed professional uneasiness and unappeased ambitions. Like Francis Wayland, Charles Hodge,

Enoch Pond, or Bennet Tyler, the orthodox were likely to decide that they could be of more service in colleges and divinity schools; similarly, Bushnell began his pastorate with the hope of an eventual professorship. Throughout the first half of the century Unitarian clergymen resigned over the protests of their congregations. In his West Roxbury parish, Theodore Parker decided he was "wasting" his "one talent," while Orville Dewey regretted that he had not become a lawyer. Things had come to such a pass that Gardiner Spring lamented that many men considered the ministry a loss of caste.[4]

What, then, were the minister's opportunities? Given the time, his most inviting prospects seemed to lie on the far side of successful talk. For to many the era seemed to be "The Golden Age of American Oratory."[5] An insatiable eagerness for instruction, rebuke, self-improvement, and reform, drove the public to lyceums and lecture halls. The people paid large sums to popular speakers; they even flocked to hear them, asking only eloquence from reformers, redeemed drunkards, Congressmen, and transcendentalists. Orators who met their needs were rewarded with attention, sometimes tears, and fame. "The highest bribes of society are at the feet of the successful orator," Emerson observed, and the theme of eloquence ran insistently through his private and published writings. In every audience he found a "capacity of virtue." Waiting on the lecturer, they were ready "to be beatified."[6]

Articles and books on homiletics constantly assured ministers that they could win the honor and power due to eloquence. The susceptible and attendant multitude, promised the *Biblical Repository*, stood "ready to swallow anything that comes in the shape of rhetoric." Nonetheless, everyone nervously continued to caution and advise the minister; he should not talk long—though political orations lasted for hours; he should avoid monotony, theology, repetition. Eventually Emerson despaired, deciding that the lecture platform made all other "pulpits" "tame and ineffectual." Not the minister but the lecturer was free to "lay himself out utterly, large, enormous, prodigal on the subject of the hour." Only on the lecture platform could he "dare to hope for ecstasy and eloquence."[7]

Undoubtedly a numerous and eager public existed. Yet, as it emerged in the writings of divines, the image of the new, knowledgeable democracy, which heard so many orators and perused so many newspapers, seemed to have been shaped in terror. Quickly bored, the public wanted novelty, action, and excitement. The conservative *Christian Observatory* warned that "a great speech in Congress, a new steamboat, . . . improvements in machinery" speedily eclipsed the people's interest in the pulpit.[8]

Ministers hazarded various expedients to win the finicky attention of the public. The *Christian Spectator* took heart at a periodical which would publish sermons right after delivery, for a sermon that came "literally smoking from the press" was far more exciting than one which had lain unpublished "even for a month." Other people counseled the worried ministry to engage in controversy. "Argument made red-hot, is what interests people," promised James Alexander.[9]

But though everyone agreed that sermons should turn on timely issues, it was hard to find any in which the public would tolerate clerical meddling. By the 1830's politics was reserved for secular oratory, while "red-hot" controversy was taken as a sign of poor taste.[10] Bushnell later regretted his abusive polemic against Bishop Brownell and wished he had not written it. The tone of his attack required an audience more concerned with theology than with gentility, and such audiences were disappearing from respectable society.

Even the minister's dominion over morals was called in question. Clergymen were admitted to reform associations, according to Gardiner Spring, rather to increase contributions than to join in serious decisions, and by the 1840's laymen dominated most "moral" societies.[11]

Within a sphere thus narrowly circumscribed, the minister had to save his congregation from tedium and himself from anonymity. "What have I done in these thirty-eight years but grow old?" Bushnell asked on his thirty-eighth birthday. During the 1830's and 1840's he struggled to find a decisive and effective role. A strange throat trouble intermittently forced him to leave his pulpit, and he pondered whether he had received a Providential decree to change his calling. Neither serenity, position, nor influence came easily to a Connecticut minister brusque in manners and unskilled in revivals.[12]

During the first decades of his ministry Bushnell alternately strained against and accepted the confines of public tolerance. He assumed the mien and duties of a Hebraic prophet; he briefly took on the political prerogatives which Puritan New England had once granted its clergy; he tried his hand at the activism of the Protestant Alliance and led a fierce war against Catholicism. All these forays after success and self-realization were executed with a sense of the times and under the tension of an obscure yet oppressive sense of the imperatives of his calling.

In these early years the young minister concerned himself with topics of general interest. Planning his first book, he proposed to study the "foundation of civil obligation" and the objects and duties of the state. At a time when politics intrigued Americans more than theology did, De Tocqueville, noting that ministers praised religion for its public utility, wondered whether the politician would supplant the priest in the young republic. Bushnell, like Beecher, Hawes, and Francis Wayland, based the case for religion on a patriotic appeal. "The divorce of politics from conscience and religion . . . must infallibly end . . . in the total wreck of our institutions and liberties," he warned. In the rhetoric of Bushnell's exuberant nationalism, the causes of America and religion became identified. His sermon *The Crisis of the Church* warned not only America of her perils but God of His, closing with a strenuous invocation. "Rise then O Men of Christ! And Thou O God of the land, arise! Fire in us the spirit of our fathers! . . . TILL OUR COUNTRY AND THY GLORY ARE SAFE!"[13]

Convinced that society and government were founded in God's decree, Bushnell criticized the social contract theory that lay behind the American Constitution and the more recent triumph of the Democrats in Connecticut. Denying the sovereign "rights of the people," Bushnell announced that an organic social order preceded and determined any written covenant. Men never existed in a Lockean "state of nature," with rights they could insure by compact, and they should therefore accept the status quo that Providence had established. Against militant Jacksonian individualism, Bushnell, like most of the northern ministry, sanctioned political conservatism.[14]

Yet Bushnell did not always identify political virtue and established power. At times, viewing man's depravity and the absolute ethic of goodness, he despaired of any political righteousness. In the height of the enthusiasm of Whigs and Democrats for the "people" and "democracy" in the 1840 campaign, Bushnell suddenly condemned politics and dared to rest his case upon a condemnation of man. The roles of Pilate and of the mob in the Crucifixion demonstrated that man "is fallen and unholy, everywhere." Democracies as well as monarchies, Bushnell intrepidly announced, were corrupted by the radical, inordinate greed of men. All principalities were "cruel, and treacherous and violent, and unfit to be trusted," for no checks could "tame" man, no balances could keep him "in the sacred bonds of order."[15]

Bushnell's revulsion at the shenanigans of the 1840 campaign, and his Calvinist mistrust of man did not usually dampen his hope for a perfect society, however. He criticized the political theory behind the Constitution as that of a government based on a balance of self-interests and therefore lost to corruption. Against the selfish atomism of checks and balances, he counterposed the hope of a Holy Commonwealth, in which legislation would insure the virtue of the state. Endowed with knowledge of the moral law, free to seek its fulfilment, Americans could aim for a perfect society. "We are fighting ourselves up up into redemption."[16]

Bushnell's Puritan conviction that the ministry should guide the state stood behind his vision of a Holy Community. In 1844 he once again broke the protocol of political silence that sealed the lips of the ministry. Perhaps, he remarked, his congregation would resent his presumption; he felt he had no choice. His duty commanded him to assert the law of God by which his hearers would face judgment. In the tones of a Hebraic prophet, he condemned the people for their political iniquities and called them to righteousness, "that the holy One of Israel may not cease from before you." An articulate and exacting ministry was essential for a virtuous nation. Piercing and announcing the divine law, the clergy could lead the people into a holy republic.[17]

Yet Bushnell was ready to compromise with the status quo when a virtuous rebellion endangered order. The structure of power registered Providential decrees, against which it would be sinful folly for individuals, the disfranchised poor, or moral associations to struggle. Thus Bushnell refused to submit the slavery question to the rashness of the human conscience. He asked only that his people acknowledge the sin of slavery and await the operation of God's will. Though in 1854 he protested against the Kansas-Nebraska compromise, since principles of right "might as well be settled by a raffle as a vote," in 1860 he still deplored human interference with slavery. He pointed to the census to demonstrate that the laws of population would peacefully eradicate slavery in God's good time.[18]

In the last analysis, Bushnell was unprepared and the people were unwilling to have the ministry act as political monitors. His *Politics under the Law of God*, used as a campaign document against the Whigs in 1844, brought such opprobrium upon Bushnell that in self-defense he published it, protesting that it had been "denounced for qualities . . . dishonorable to a minister."[19] For the next decade he said nothing about politics. Except for a denunciation of the Kansas-Nebraska Act, he maintained his silence, until the Civil War. Only then, when the exigencies of conflict made ministerial support welcome to the public, did Bushnell again essay the role of prophet and political mentor.

Bushnell had not found a role answering his sense of vocation. Throughout the 1840's he painfully deliberated the advisability of remaining in the ministry. Offered the presidency of Middlebury College in 1840, he found the decision difficult. He could not decipher the call of duty. His wife apparently preferred to stay in Hartford, and his own eagerness to advance "his mind and studies" at Middlebury warred with other, less articulate attachments. After he rejected the position, he continued to be tempted by hopes of greater freedom and a wider field. In 1842 and 1843 he made a brief lecturing tour in New York, Connecticut, and Ohio and wondered whether his "peculiarities of thinking and style" were not more suited to the West than to the East. The West, he enthusiastically reported, was hospitable to originality; clearly he had felt constrained in the unbending East.[20]

During his forties Bushnell remained unsure where to direct his ambition and energy. Everywhere the church seemed weakened. In the rapid increase of voluntary societies, he gloomily noted the dwindling role of the church, of the ministry, and of Christian affections. He resented the reversal of the moral order of New England Calvinism. Joining anti-tobacco, anti-alcohol, and anti-slavery societies, laymen, filled with "conceit of their own superior wisdom," accused the clergy of moral laxity.[21] Meanwhile, in Catholicism, Bushnell saw not only Protestantism but America itself imperiled.

He turned increasingly upon this enemy and entered a battle that joined the political and social fears of the nation with the aims of the Protestant ministry. In 1843 he, with Beecher, Hawes, and other ministers of Connecticut, formed the Protestant League to overthrow the papacy. As Bushnell pointed out to Leonard Bacon, the vast scope of the project would obliterate religious differences. Should the Catholics launch a counteroffensive, "even the wicked" in America would spring to defend Protestantism, led by a clergy they otherwise ignored.[22]

Bushnell sponsored the Alliance with great expectations. He fought for a union without creeds, bound together by a common plan of action. Without a practical purpose, as New England's religious history demonstrated, all Christian undertakings collapsed. The Alliance portended a new era in which there would be no schisms and no enforced belief, but the comprehensiveness of a universal church. For at last religion had an ally in the age. Jubilantly, Bushnell announced that at this point religion could turn the "very laws of human society" to its account. Religion could maintain itself not by judgment upon history but only in accommodation to historical forces. "Who," Bushnell jubilantly asked, "will dread a failure, when the laws of society are with him?"[23]

Beyond the aim of religious liberty and Protestant unity, the Alliance had little coherence, but it gave Bushnell a focus for his energy and hopes. He addressed large audiences on the subject in New York and Boston, and in Europe he wrote an open letter to the Pope, demanding religious liberty for Catholics. In England his connection with the Alliance saved him from total isolation.

The Alliance sent Bushnell to London as its representative at an international meeting in 1847. But, displeased that the international group excluded slaveholders and included Episcopalians, and indignant that it set creedal requirements for members, Bushnell lost interest in the project and turned to the simpler task of saving America from Catholicism. In 1847 he urged the Home Missionary Society that the West had to be redeemed "from above" (i.e., by the East), to be saved from slavery, Catholicism, and barbarism. The address won him a national reputation and the applause of the conservative *Biblical Repository*. He seemed to be following the path Lyman Beecher had so successfully opened in his *Plea for the West*.[24]

Even in the midst of his Alliance activities, however, Bushnell was obsessed with alien problems. His only son had died in 1842. In his need, Bushnell turned to pietistic writings. If he soon shook off his quietism for "a broader, more positive state," a new vision of Christian life remained to disturb and tempt him. In his church he pictured the sanctification of "pure love" that was achieved by submission to pain. Such a love conquered by the mortification of the will, not by a strategic alliance with the world, but as Bushnell disciplined himself in suffering, it seemed to contain the essence of the Gospel. On a morning in 1848 he had a vision of Christianity.[25]

To seek Christ with personal intensity, to look for truth in Catholic pietists, to have had a vision, were poor qualifications for the systematized business of Protestant benevolence and aggression. That fatal instability which led Bushnell to religious ecstasy sealed his destiny. He could not, like Beecher, fling himself into moral evangelism. He was unable to win pre-eminence, as Bacon was doing, by domination of associations. In his short, fragmentary autobiography Bushnell took time to mention that he was never chosen to be president or vice-president of any society and was almost never asked to be on a committee. "I was looked upon as a singularity—not exactly sane, perhaps in many things. . . . Take the report of my doings on the platform of the world's business, and it is naught. I have filled no place at all."[26]

Yet he was gaining a reputation as a public speaker. The Unitarian *Christian Examiner* and the orthodox *Biblical Repository* praised his sure eloquence, while the *Princeton Review* dolefully noted that his heresies received attention because of his prodigious eloquence, which made him a popular speaker for an "occasion" and tempted him to a feckless originality. By 1851, the year when a history of Litchfield County was published, Bushnell's fame was established as having "delivered more orations and discourses on anniversary occasions, than any other New England clergyman."[27]

His genius as well as his circumstances forced him back upon eloquence, upon language, even upon theology. He came to think of his lifework in terms of the message he had been called to deliver. Driven by some need for Christian identification, he seemed to seek persecution. Pondering heresy, he quickened his courage by the thought of Luther. As the shadow of consumption lengthened over him, he used the prospect of death to force himself to speak quickly the truth he had glimpsed.[28]

When Bushnell turned to religious questions, he was troubled by the problem of communication. From the first, he longed to address a wider audience than Congregationalist Hartford or Connecticut. The truth seemed to him manifold; theological accusations were provincial and in poor taste, as the Unitarians had pointed out; worse, they shut the broad truth within a narrow sphere.

In the 1840's Bushnell was tapping at the door of enlightened Boston. He hobnobbed briefly with Parker and Ripley and formed a lasting friendship with Unitarian Cyrus Bartol. In 1847 he assured Bartol that the split between orthodoxy and Unitarians was not a serious one and that he could state his own orthodoxy in terms that Unitarians would approve. With the invitation to address the Harvard Divinity School, he had his chance to try. It was a pregnant opportunity. Bushnell knew the Unitarians were watching him; according to the orthodox Enoch Pond, it was common knowledge that he was a "prominent candidate" for the Hollis Chair at Harvard.[29]

Bushnell could not afford to let his distinguished audience depart without the ecstasy won by eloquence. But communication across the distance between Hartford Congregationalism and Boston Unitarianism would test the resources of the most skilful speaker. If such communication required a catholic tone, only an inspired originality could distinguish the occasion.

At least Bushnell was used to worrying about eloquence; for years he had pursued the secret of successful language. In Europe and England he had scrutinized the techniques of preachers; if in France he discovered a preacher more "elegant" than himself, he took comfort in his rival's relative inertia. Inspecting another French minister, he decided that "short rapid gestures from the elbow cannot be connected with great depth of sentiment." His final criticism of Swedenborgianism was that it could not be preached effectively, for it would not inflame the heart.[30]

Political prophecy and moral activism had not met Bushnell's needs; oratory furnished a more propitious trial. Most of his published works before 1860 had first been spoken. In a time when one of the nation's most successful authors defined a writer as an *"orateur manqué"* literary patterns were likely to be designed to meet the requirements of oratory.[31] The spoken discourse had become the accepted form of non-fictional popular literature, and the eloquence, which articles assiduously analyzed, informed the prose of Emerson, Thoreau, Parker, and Bushnell. Seeking consent from audiences adequately equipped for judgment, the speaker, as later the writer, was proved by his success.

Probation by oratory seemed the corollary of democracy. Isolated in his study, the minister knew nothing of the people. Face to face with the audience he must win, the speaker alone took the pulse of the nation and mastered the strategy of persuasion. American theologians largely agreed that the theology "best fitted to be preached" was "on that account most entitled to be believed." "Hence," enthused the *Bibliotheca Sacra*, "our bodies of divinity are living . . . ; the soul of them is still eloquent."[32]

Thus the question circled back to eloquence. Its power alone could reaffirm the flagging ascendancy of the word of God. Ministers avidly searched out the mysteries of "pulpit eloquence" in quest of the touch that could beatify. They conned the models of success and exhaustively analyzed the predilections of the sovereign public. "So fleeting as it is," mused Emerson, "yet what is so excellent of present Power as the riding this wild horse of the People!"[33]

Bushnell decided his role and techniques in the shared

context of his colleagues' anxiety and ambitions. He was bound by the discipline of contemporary eloquence. During the 1840's the logic and form of his works derived from the grammar of successful oratory. Gradually he shaped an image of himself from the new mirror for the ministry which desperate yet sanguine men constructed from the necessities of the time.

In the model of the minister little trace remained of the Calvinist teacher instructing a hungry flock in the Gospel. The minister sounded more like the popular orator. William Russell's "ideal preacher" was a familiar figure. "Persuasion dwells on the very accents of his voice; he seems to mould the mind at will." Level with his audience, surrounded by a host of faces, the minister could make the crowd the instrument of his feeling. Such was the power of true eloquence that the congregation could be "fused," "electrified," "melted" into union.[34]

But for success, the minister had to avoid protracted logic. Few people cared to follow intricate arguments. Republicans, Henry Ripley announced, were not thinkers, readers, or scholars, and the minister should adjust himself to their limitations. Similarly, the *New Englander* warned that democracy, disliking "labored" reasoning, could not "wait long" for the truth. Eloquence submerged art and order in a "whirlpool of excited feeling," where the mind rushed head-on to truths and passionate feelings. Finding himself too illogical for the law, the imaginative young Emerson hoped to thrive in divinity, while Bushnell waited anxiously for inspiration which "set everything gliding and flowing, whether to order or not."[35]

As deadly as the dragging pace of logic was its interference with sudden revelations. Logic was equated with tradition, and religious periodicals conceded that the public was tired of conventional theology. The "people" were waiting for unwonted ideas. Advised by such reputable periodicals as the *New Englander* to avoid the "stereotyped forms of sound words" and to offer instead an "unusual exhibition," the minister had to exploit idiosyncratic inspirations. Only in spontaneous discourses, which to the "mere theologian" might seem a "wilderness of confusion," could the audience be pierced by inspiration, and the *Biblical Repository* guaranteed that the congregation of an "awakened spirit" would stay awake for fear of missing his "fireworks."[36]

By 1857 it was clear that in Henry Ward Beecher the categories of eloquence had found fulfilment. His thoughts moved "in shocks rather than sentences." Whether listeners understood or not, they responded. With his materials "loosely tacked together," Beecher caught their attention and inspired their devotion. Struck by his matchless success, Bushnell told Andover students that the ideal of the preacher had henceforward to be revised.[37]

Eloquence required a spontaneous disorder broken by sudden revelations, and Bushnell, who in his early years had done much patient "digging" to find anything "fresh" in the theme of Christ, searched for his own unique message with relentless desperation. Describing the operation of grace, he could find no word but inspiration. Faith was a "supernatural beholding," giving men knowledge beyond logical demonstration. Preaching seemed to him the "bursting out of light," and reviewers praised him for the startling insights that his logic did not always sustain. As the model of preacher-orator incited his ambition, a certain looseness entered the processes of his thought. Yet if he disdained and avoided any close, foolish consistency, he exacted an unfailing originality of himself. Of the two, the latter obligation may well have been the more burdensome.[38]

The revolt against the priestly office, the contempt for logical structure and traditional ideas, put new pressures on

the minister. Once tradition and faith had carried the weight
of argument; now it rested heavily upon the individual. The
minister spoke increasingly as a person without investiture,
requesting the attention of other people. Audiences waited,
hoping to be moved, desiring the shock of witnessed faith.
Their hunger pushed the preacher to personal exploitation.
Henry Ward Beecher explained that people flocked to his
church for the same reason that they went to Barnum's
museum; other preachers, schooled to a more exigent sense
of their calling, carried an oppressive burden. "The teacher
should be as near like a seraph as possible. He should mount
the chariot of Amnadab—the fiery chariot of Elijah," Kirk
enjoined. Bushnell accepted the exorbitant injunction. The
minister had to reincarnate the Gospel, for mere theories
were impotent. Other men could receive God only if He
were expressed "in the face and words and thoughts and acts
of a man."[39] If the aim was presumptuous, it must also have
been unnerving.

Yet even if the minister was a seraph, he was not to act
as a judge—eloquence had to observe the proprieties. Not
even the most inspired disorder could insure the successful
pronouncement of evangelical faith; during the nineteenth
century, articles increasingly resorted to such adjectives as
"rude," "coarse," and "barbarous" to describe the basic
tenets of Calvinism. By the 1840's, it seemed clear that New
England Congregationalism had been guilty of indiscretions;
its theology seemed "unrefined," its worship "rude and un-
graceful." Unfortunately, New England divines had too
often disdained the "ornaments of refined sensibility" and
"the graces of life," confessed the *Biblical Repository*.[40]

At a time when the middle classes were nervously pursu-
ing gentility, Calvinism was being identified with poor taste.
The earlier expansion of Unitarianism in Massachusetts enforced an ominous lesson, and Unitarians complacently

harped upon the inevitable "aversion of men of taste to evangelical religion." In nineteenth-century Connecticut, Episcopalianism was luring away the "better classes of society." In 1844, Andover's Edwards Park reported that modern politeness found Congregationalism "clumsy" and that young men "of taste" were seeking other churches.[41]

The signal mark of departing parishioners seemed to be the "refined and poetic feeling" which the *Christian Spectator* saw as the key to upper-class society. Surveying the public, the *New Englander* discerned a vast assembly engaged in "elegant" reading; such readers were at once so "influential" and so touchy that the Unitarian *Christian Examiner* excused unusual ministerial gentleness before them. Reluctant to part with such promising parishioners, Congregationalists accepted the need for doctrinal accommodations. "We cannot allow to Unitarians," the *New Englander* protested, "the monopoly of all the outward graces of religion," or concede that Unitarianism alone could "refine and elevate."[42]

Before the Calvinist God all men were equally sinners, whose major need was to know their guilt and impotence, and whose sole hope was a free, unmerited gift of grace. But the nineteenth-century man of taste did not fit into the democracy of universal depravity, being, in the view of the *Christian Spectator*, more accessible to the Gospel than the common herd. For the conversion of so sensitive a being, the *Bibliotheca Sacra* advised against denunciation and recommended a "gentlemanly address" to his conscience and feelings. Sharp recriminations were unnecessary, and the *Biblical Repository*, conceding that Christ had treated the Pharisees harshly, concluded that America had no such reprobates and cautioned the minister to please the "tasteful and erudite." Taste was becoming the arbiter of theology; in 1850 Edwards Park warned that the minister who failed to inspire "choice men and women" and whose doctrines grated against "refined sentiments" had clearly erred in theology.[43]

Religious articles and gift books insisted that religion did not violate but fulfilled the imperatives of sensibility. The *Christian Keepsake* was founded to demonstrate that "some of the Muse's most fragrant flowers bloom on Zion's hill," while the *Biblical Repository* urged that the "winged words" of poetry could best overleap the dilemmas of theology. Though the point was not easily won, religious writers hammered diligently on the theme of the alliance of poetry and religion.[44]

Bushnell, too, celebrated the marriage of religion and taste and rejoiced that the urban East, casting off the "rudeness" of early Calvinism, was modifying religion by the "softer shades of feeling." Taste, he announced, made men like God. For while the metaphysician dragged himself along by a "cold, defining process," the poet discerned "images of truth." Though logic was futile, by grace of taste, men might find God.[45]

Thus, religious truth no longer needed to wait upon the thumping verdicts of common sense but might politely call upon the delicate responsiveness of "congenial feeling." The romantic guide to eloquence promised escape from the ennui of logic, the crudeness of accusation, the isolation of withheld assent. The work of poet and orator fused. Both sought to communicate emotion; both avoided abstractions and logic; both "painted to the bodily eye." The orator, Bushnell concluded, was "a free lyric in his own living person."[46]

But the refinements of eloquence were costly, and the methods and doctrines of the people's inherited faith were the price. To Edwards Park at Andover, the tensions between eloquence and tradition split theology itself in half. To an enthusiastic Boston audience Park described the disparate qualities of "The Theology of the Intellect and of the Feelings." The theology of the intellect excelled in "controversial treatises and bodies of divinity" but bored most people. Eloquence dwelt with the "theology of the heart," which gratified the sensibility. "An outpouring of sentiments too deep, or too mellow, or too impetuous to be suited with the stiff language of the intellect," the theology of the feelings achieved the spontaneity of nature. Truths too "spiritual and refined" for the intellect were the stuff of eloquence. The inventive poetic faculty, bringing forth "symbol after symbol," could alone inspire and move the heart.[47]

The canons for eloquence undermined traditional religion. Invited to lecture at the Harvard Divinity School, at Andover, and at Yale in 1848, Bushnell was brought sharply up against the problem of effective religious address. Seeking to reach "that class of men" who entered theology from its "esthetic side," he inevitably aspired to eloquence. *God in Christ* attempted to show "that the advancement and real amount of true theology" depended "not on logical deductions . . . but . . . on the more cultivated and nicer apprehension of symbol."[48]

But Bushnell could not stop short with the eloquence of the feelings, with the admired *non sequiturs* of a Henry Ward Beecher, or with the nebulous effusions of the gift books. He did not slur over the revision implicit in the definitions of eloquence but met the contemporary sensibility with a proposal to unite the theology of intellect and feeling through a new understanding of language.

The lectures which later became *God in Christ* assigned theology a new role: properly interpreted, theology was poetry, suited to the finest minds; no longer the domain of unremitting logic, it became the very instrument of eloquence. To the lectures thus interpreting Christian dogma, Bushnell prefaced a treatise on language. Contemporaries had provided a compendious manual on oratorical know-how; Bushnell investigated the relation of religious truth to the premises and nature of effective language. The love for coherence was inherent in the New England tradition; Bushnell's need to analyze and comprehend proved stronger than his rejection of New England's provincial rationalism.

Yet the pursuit of eloquence was so pervasive that its problems preoccupied his mind. Even for Bushnell, who faced the issues more squarely than mose of his contemporaries, the obsession with effective oratory obscured the degree of New England's religious crisis. As early as 1839 he identified the achievement of eloquence with knowledge of the truth. Was it merely a matter of discovering the techniques of eloquence, or was it a problem of religious knowledge that could shatter certainty at its base? The question was to hover behind *God in Christ* without finding final resolution.

Insistently, relentlessly, the contemporary sensibility made its demands. Audiences who crowded lyceums and sighed over gift books displayed their boredom, their complacency, their refinement, in the church, yet waited, there as elsewhere, for beatitude. To the orator, Bushnell decided, belonged "a power sublime above all others possible to man."[49] Yet, unlike Henry Ward Beecher, Bushnell could not merely ride the top waves of the public's confusion. Some obstinate curiosity, born with his peculiar, visionary faith and nursed even in the rebellious years under Nathaniel Taylor, forced him to seek understanding of the ethos he accepted.

VII. The Experience of Words

From his first costly discovery of the gap between cultivated and rural speech, the problem of language dogged Bushnell. Dependent upon eloquence for success, he faced a public that found theology tedious and considered Calvinistic terminology, like rustic dialect, to be boorish. Within his profession and his faith, Bushnell had to discover a message adapted to his concern for belief and the public's demand for eloquence.

A sudden multiplication of opportunities in the 1840's focused his necessity and ambition. He found himself no longer addressing the limited Hartford audience. He had friends in Boston, the center of cultivated eloquence and of Unitarian liberalism. In the 1848 invitation to address the Harvard Divinity School, he witnessed a "providential" intervention aimed at union between enlightened Congregationalism and Unitarianism. He sensed that a crisis in his career was at hand, and he awaited its outcome exuberantly. He welcomed the chance to preach in Boston for Cyrus Bartol; explaining to his friend that he might well be displaced for his forthcoming heresies, he mentioned his interest in "a place somewhere" and suggested that Dr. Lowell might accept a colleague.[1] In addition, there beckoned the honor of the Hollis Chair. Yet, in seizing the occasion, Bushnell had to call upon the reviled theology of Trinitarian

Calvinism. He was anxious to please Unitarian Boston, but he was crusading in behalf of his non-Unitarian faith.

To meet the exigency of these promising years, Bushnell turned to ideas he had been privately considering for almost a decade. As early as 1839 he had decided that he was ready to publish a "heresy" on the Trinity which would "make a little breeze." "To withhold longer," he feared, would betray a "want of that moral courage which animated Luther and every other man who has been a soldier of Christ."[2] He had already come to conceive of himself as a rebel graced by private illuminations. Still, it was nine years before Bushnell, encouraged by Unitarian advances, publicly expounded his insights. In 1848 he announced his theories before the Harvard Divinity School, at Andover, and at Yale.

A year later Bushnell published the addresses in *God in Christ*, adding a prefatory treatise on language. The Preface dealt with familiar concerns: the relations between words and reality. It proposed that only a revised conception of the common medium of the orator and the theologian could finally join eloquence, truth, and theology.

Behind the Preface stood the changing society, the skepticism, and new faiths of the time, which had turned language, once unquestioned, into something problematic. An increasing divergence between tradition and credence made the religious vocabulary of the past sound archaic and unconvincing. The search for semantic understanding, the fear of the "artifice" of abstraction, were not peculiar to Bushnell; from Moses Stuart to Emerson, religious men dreaded the unreality of words and searched for a new language that would prove both true and powerful. On every side the problem loomed: in the common-sense philosophy, in Unitarian rationalism, in the beginnings of science and textual criticism. In what sense, if any, could theology pretend to be knowledge?

94

The difficulty was deep-rooted. Frequently, *Hints to Sunday School Teachers* lamented, "very good people" betrayed an aversion to a "religious, Christian dialect."[3] In spite of the electricity of sympathy, the jolts of unstraitened inspiration, the seraphic glance of the orator, eloquence at some point had to resort to words. Here trouble began. The people craved to listen; yet never had language seemed less substantial to those who preached the Word of God.

The Word itself, newly subjected to textual study, had revealed dismaying ambiguities. After 1810, Moses Stuart initiated Andover students into the mysteries of Hebrew points and exhorted them to single-minded pursuit of the literal meaning of the text. Yet, read without the distortions of theology or "metaphysical subtleties," the Bible proved a shaking document. Established interpretations of crucial passages were uprooted; creeds became uncertain; the structure of Divinity was imperiled at its base. Even the creed of Trinitarianism emerged as "artifact," which no church should force upon believers. From the authority of his assiduous research, Stuart announced the frailty of language. "Things, not mere words, belong to the essence of the Christian creed."[4]

Stuart's esoteric knowledge was carried into the back country by the *Bibliotheca Sacra* and the *Biblical Repository* and by bumptious Andover graduates who appalled examining councils by their disdain for "secondary" meanings and by their easy dismissal of proof-texts, through which the faith had been defended for generations.[5] The Bible itself thus undermined New England's religious tradition.

The Unitarians were also taking refuge from distasteful doctrines in the Bible, but, unlike Stuart, they were not content with baffled awe before its "facts." Reading the text with discrimination, they found it a compilation of chaos— the barbarities of an ancient time mixed with a lofty ethic, lasting truths joined to excessive exuberance. Composed in remote and ignorant times, the Bible required stringent interpretation of the letter by the spirit. The understanding was final judge, for God would not confound the reason which was His primary gift to man. "If religion be the shipwreck of the understanding," Channing announced, "we can not keep too far from it."[6]

The attack against the Trinity began there. The concept of three gods made inordinate demands upon the reason and distracted the mind by its unseemly display of "a bleeding, suffering God." Calvinism had yoked man under a "legislation unspeakably dreadful, under laws written, like Draco's, in blood"; Unitarianism proposed for his considered obedience the serenity of "a rational and amiable system." Christ was the easiest of all historical characters to understand, and his service consisted in the simple lessons of his example and teaching. Channing warned the preacher agaibt lavishing superstitious adoration upon his person. Properly, the minister taught Christ's beliefs.[7]

Lucid and undismayed, human intelligence stood at the center of Unitarian Christianity. "Strange would it be," Orville Dewey wrote, "if, in a religion so simple and reasonable as ours, that on which everything in our moral welfare hangs, should be a mystery." The Bible itself had to be pruned by the enlightened mind. Guilty of enthusiasm, ecstasy, and poetry, the Bible required skilled excisions. According to Andrews Norton, only the theologian was equipped to disentangle the "literal meanings" of the text from the metaphors and images which obscured significance. The scholar alone, with more discretion than the Bible, could reason with words as if they were "algebraic symbols" and at the end of his algebra could point to a proposition that common sense could assess.[8] For, if poetry and language seemed ambiguous to Unitarians, they knew that good sense could speedily discern the truth.

Meanwhile the new science of geology was similarly challenging Biblical prose. Under any of the going geological theories, Genesis stood in need of reinterpretation. Much in Unitarian style, orthodox scientist Benjamin Silliman disposed of the Bible's factual inaccuracies by praising it as a code of moral instruction adapted to primitive ignorance. In lyceums, Amherst lectures, and articles, Silliman's pupil Hitchcock stressed that the "gross descriptions" of the Bible were useful for the masses, while the elite could seek its true propositions beneath its obfuscating imagery.[9]

By the 1840's the terminology of theology and revelation itself had been set in question by the requirements of reason. Acceptable keys to meaning lay in scientific discoveries and in the moral intuitions of common sense; for the rest, as Stuart seemed to imply, there was no meaning beyond Biblical fact. Behind immediate perplexities and maneuvers stood the larger question of the relation of language to the truth. But if the difficulty required a semantic, and if religious periodicals vaguely responded by articles on philology, hermeneutics, and remote languages, public interest did not follow the problem to that extremity.

Connecticut Congregationalists avoided the intricacies of Hebrew points and metaphors largely by ignoring the issue. At Yale, Nathaniel Taylor stoutly announced that words were the "signs of things." For meaning, words depended upon the incommunicable simple ideas, which, as Locke had taught, were the materials of all knowledge. Since all complex ideas could be broken down into their constituent simple ideas, meaning could be precise. Metaphysical puzzles resulted from the failure to pin down definitions to internal or external perceptions.[10]

Yet first Locke and later his Scottish and American fol-

lowers noted the difficulty of communicating internal perceptions, since such words could not indicate any common
or "external" data. The language devised for this extremity
revealed man's drastic dependence upon sensations, for he
described the operations of his soul by metaphors derived
from perceptions. According to Stewart and Campbell, an
investigation of any language would prove that "all words"
denoting "spiritual and intellectual things" were taken from
objects of sense.[11]

Convinced that perceptions furnished the wherewithal of
knowledge, the Scottish philosophers saw no crucial role
for language. The images used for describing subjective experiences were misleading, and Blair hoped that eventually
metaphors and imagination would disappear, as intellectual
progress made language more precise. Analogical reasoning
was totally fallacious. Ideally, philosophical language was
abstract and free from the distracting suggestiveness of
tropes. It was so clear that an algebra of reasoning could be
conducted without reference to the perceived world, until
the simple, sensed datum was pointed to in proof of the
validity of the argument.[12]

Yet knowing man to be a creature of the senses, Scottish
philosophers made no promise that abstractions would fasci-
nate an audience. From the security of an endowed chair at
Harvard, Andrews Norton might seek an austere algebraic
truth, but ministers longing for an audience could not so
easily dismiss the human weaknesses that complacently
judged them. Before ambitious sacred orators, the Scottish
philosophers set the bleak alternatives of a tedious soundness
or a specious appeal.

Only figurative language, it seemed, could call into play
the "early associations" which were so powerful a weapon
of the poet or orator. Common-sense philosophers urged
speakers to evoke the reality of things, since, as Timothy

Dwight announced, all men knew that "the objects of our senses" impressed the mind far more than "those of the understanding." Constructed from perceptions, abstractions lacked force; to Lord Kames they seemed too "faint and obscure" to move the heart.[13] Because only the vividness of things could arrest the audience, metaphors, images, and "word pictures" were the tools of eloquence.

Though the Scottish philosophers had only casually explored the techniques of oratory, Americans seized upon their directives and dinned the lesson of concreteness into prospective orators. "Is there aught in eloquence which warms the heart?" inquired Samson Reed. "She draws her fire from natural imagery." The *Christian Spectator* warned the clergy that abstractions did not consort with eloquence. "Mere *words*" might enlighten the mind, but only images could enflame the heart. "The great law of popular and effective speaking," Bushnell told Andover students, is "concinnity," "agreeing figures and associations." But to Bushnell, as early as 1839, the device of effective speaking had become the law of popular truth.[14]

If the longing for eloquence turned Americans from algebra to tropes, they could argue nevertheless that empiricism itself undermined abstractions. If the final elements of knowledge were simple perceptions, which were linked together by habitual association, empiricism offered no basis for faith but custom. Salvation, truth, God, redemption, were artifacts constructed of, and reducible to, multiple sensations. Bushnell read the results of a rigorous sensationalism in A. B. Johnson's book on words and things, which stressed that the sole function of words was to "refer us to phenomena." Each word meant only the distinct "sights, tastes, sounds, and smells" which it lumped together in factitious unity; experience guaranteed no sequence or relation but the chaos of discrete sensations; and language that could not

99

point to sense data was gibberish. Under such strict empiricism, intellectual meanings threatened to evaporate.[15] Symbols were signs of things and were justified by the sensible reality they indicated.

Though the circle was constricting, philosophy seemed to offer no broader arena. Dedicated to the destruction of the "artifices" of society and history, Americans could not content themselves with the artifice of abstractions; eventually a peculiarly national escape was won. The society that had obliterated the artificial aristocracies of the Old World turned to the nature of man, which the democracy trusted, and to the vast American nature, which senators and artists were celebrating, for release from philosophical stultification. Emerson noted that the mind spontaneously turned from the "rotten diction" of abstraction to the reality of things. "The moment our discourse . . . is inflamed with passion or exalted by thought, it clothes itself with images." At Andover, Ebenezer Porter rejoiced that man instinctively thought by images, thus escaping the insubstantiality of "mere *words*," while at Yale, Bushnell had heard Josiah Gibbs announce that all language was rooted in physical meanings by a "perceived analogy."[16]

The democracy was ready to trust the instinctive operations of the human mind. Americans did not attend to Scottish warnings against delusive analogies; instead, they took hope for religion and oratory in the pervasive imagery of nature. Nature offered man the concrete tongue of metaphor by divine decree. Even as a student Bushnell had seen proof of God in the natural symbols which man spontaneously turned into metaphors. In 1835, the *Biblical Repository* urged ministers to study nature, since the world was so filled with spiritual meanings that every particle of it furnished a "true and appropriate symbol," and Bushnell in 1839 pointed out to the Andover Rhetorical Society that eloquence could not fail the sacred orator, as God had provided natural forms to embody every truth.[17]

Empiricism and eloquence alike had turned Americans to metaphor; Bushnell found a new key to religion in the pervasive insistence on imagery. Because the "Logos in the outward world" corresponded with spiritual perceptions, men could apprehend and communicate religious truths. The world was a hieroglyph offered by God for the spirit's deciphering. Here the Deity, lost in a harsh theology, might be rediscovered in persuasive and amiable reality, and the preacher could hope to move the fastidious heart in the very act of speaking divine truth. *God in Christ* expanded the thesis. Every word had a physical base. Like Johnson, Bushnell insisted that the reality of language was "not in the vocal names" but in the "images they represent." But he criticized Johnson's failure to grasp the spiritual meanings that pervaded the physical. In nature, man faced God Himself. Men derived words from things not in desperation or ignorance but graced by divine illumination.[18]

True, Bushnell's faith in this divine language wavered. God communicated through metaphors, but Bushnell turned to science for promise of a language in which truth, "lying no longer in the mere superfices" would become "consistent, permanent knowledge." Like the Scottish realists and like other Americans, he anticipated the transformation of the vague realm of fancy into "distinct and certain" knowledge by the increase of empirical data, and even suggested that until scientific investigation was complete, spiritual truths could not be fully known.[19] Bushnell neither recognized nor resolved these contradictory assumptions: at times he declared that religious knowledge was given by God to the imagination in metaphors; at other times that truth was located in perceptions made exact by scientific inquiry. Though he aimed to justify transcendent faith, he shared his

101

time's uncertainties. Suspicions of the spirit and imagination craved the certitude of factual things.

Though the accepted common-sense realism gave Americans no epistemological warrant for their search for spiritual truths, winds of foreign doctrines touched American shores and lessened the logical strain. Coleridge's *Aids* had recommended that the young minister study the metaphoric significance of words and had often traced words to their root-meanings.

Yet for Coleridge words could not become the keys to final significance. To name a thing was to assign it a place in the realm of the Understanding. Reason alone confronted ineffable spiritual truths; and Coleridge turned to this higher faculty with a serenity his American followers envied but could not share. For Coleridge was not perplexed, as they perforce were, by the requirements of eloquence, and he did not turn to the reality of things with the needy insistence of men who were philosophical empiricists and professional orators.

German idealism, too, offered an escape from associationalism, but most New Englanders had only spotty contact with contemporary German thought. Bushnell, who knew no foreign tongue, was acquainted with German theology only in translation. He had read Moses Stuart's translation of Schleiermacher's analysis of Sabellianism; he knew the work of the idealist Neander, a Jew converted to Christianity by Schleiermacher, and the *Psychology* of Frederick Rauch, who taught that space and time were categories of thought, which could not be derived from experience. In England Bushnell had chatted with John Morell, who wished to center the religious life in intuitions that transcended language and form.

In the foreign writers who influenced Bushnell, certain motifs were constant. Because of the idealistic metaphysics

102

behind German speculation, the central issue concerned the relation between finite and infinite spirit. The religious crisis was enacted within the individual consciousness, not in tensions between the individual and outer reality. German idealists did not need to agitate the superior reality of things, for faith was fulfilled in the union between the individual and universal spirit. Christ, the church, language, and the Bible mediated the transition from self-will to experience of the Absolute. The religious conflict began and ended in the spirit, and different theologies were only the machinery that externalized the drama. Though forms were necessarily inaccurate, the impoverishment of language could not blur the reception of the truth, which was felt and inarticulate. "Gefühl ist alles: Name ist Schall und Rauch," Goethe had written, testifying for the epoch.[20] The German romantic conviction that spirit informed the universe was welcome to Americans, though it was a difficult concept to fit within indigenous traditions.

Lacking the metaphysical discipline behind idealism, many Americans in fact dismissed the Germans as foggy dreamers. Few ministers would have been so old-fashioned or imprudent as to delve into German metaphysics, having so recently escaped New England's. Their problems did not strike them as metaphysical. Orthodox translations of German writers concentrated upon church history or samples of the enviable eloquence that had given rebirth to German piety.

The tireless pursuit of things, of perceptive reality, of effective oratory, could not be slackened. Europeans did not resolve the dilemmas of the sacred orator; they scarcely framed the question. Schleiermacher was convinced that his preaching was more powerful when he spoke from a philosophy his hearers did not understand,[21] but such dualism was inaccessible to Americans who could not conceive a truth

103

thus alien to common sense and who, if they tried to address an elite, soon lacked an audience. The demands of eloquence plagued Congregational ministers and Boston transcendentalists alike.

Were words things and things spirit in such correspondence that the spiritual world achieved form, or did every word distort the vast fluidity of the Infinite? These were the poles of an antithesis that troubled Emerson, the young Thoreau, and Whitman as well as Bushnell. Emerson might assert that the mind necessarily took the "forms for thought" from nature; elsewhere he berated language as mere "Schall und Rauch." Words could not "cover the dimensions of what is in truth. They break, chop, and impoverish it." They were an "operose, circuitous way of putting us in mind of the thing."[22]

Bushnell, too, often described spiritual knowledge as so distinct from form that language could only distort it. The word at best pointed to the ineffable vision of the seer. Terms were "only analogies, symbols, shadows . . . of the formless mysteries above us and within us." The consciousness intuited truths, which the logical faculty bunglingly cramped into doctrines and images. Only an abundance of conflicting creeds could salvage the truth, for by embracing them all the mind avoided a falsifying precision and confronted the "interior formless nature of the truth."[23] If the truth resided in a realm where language could not penetrate, communication was a treacherous task. Still, the necessities of communication remained. An audience might easily confuse intuitions with "mere abstractions" and depart with sensibilities unmoved. Bushnell's addresses set out to solve the dilemma of eloquence, truth, and faith, to offer his hearers what Channing had required: a poetry of the soul, "borrowing form the whole outward creation fresh images and correspondences."[24]

Bushnell proposed a reading of theology which he hoped would end the bickering dogmatism of Protestantism and herald the return of an apostolic unity. The instrument of such a Christian peace was to be the aesthetic sensibility which alone avoided the sterile debates of logic and pierced to the center of faith. Christian truth itself emerged as "the expression of God—God coming into expression, through histories and rites, through an incarnation, and through language—in one syllable, by the WORD." *God in Christ* presented a new approach to Christian theology, imagery, ritual, and history. Religion was not to be probed by the understanding but apprehended by the "imaginative reason," for the effort of the Bible was "by means of expression, and under the laws of expression, to set forth God—His providence, and His government, and, what is more . . . God's own feeling, His truth, love, justice, compassion." Christian forms existed to convey the infinite truth to man's finite capacities.[25]

Bushnell defended the Trinity on the battleground the Unitarians had chosen. To him it seemed the perfect instrument of the soul's necessities, for it kept the mind straining unceasingly after God. Through the Trinity, not in abstraction from it, experience received an "algebraic" formulation which could convey transcendent mystery. The infinitude and incommensurability of God demanded paradox. Only through the Trinity could the "mysteries of law and grace, letter and spirit" enter practically into belief.[26]

Thus he challenged the premises of his Unitarian audience in his insistence on a God so hidden that the mind had to strain after Him. So inaccessible a divinity had long since departed from the liberal imagination. But for Bushnell, the soul, when searching out divine things, was properly held in a "maze," not judging God but groping toward Him through form. He kept before neglectful hearers the need to check the soul, which otherwise in its quest for God might merely discover itself. Only objective form could restrain the human egotism which would dogmatize on the Deity. Though men fancied they improved religion by extracting theory from scriptural imagery, actually there was "just as much less of solidity" in religion as there was more that was from men's selves. Symbols and ritual were necessary to carry men from their own centers; "otherwise our piety . . . settles into a mere dressing of the soul before her mirror."²⁷

Language itself was a form which saved the soul from vacuity. As the words which described the realm of spirit were images derived from nature, the "whole web of speech" was "curiously woven metaphor," offered to the imagination. Through the deciphering of the images of spiritual things, men came to know God. At times Bushnell suggested that for man there was no escape from the husk of language. Feeling was not all; it depended upon the word for its peculiar existence. In relation to religious truth, words did not merely point to a proposition or a sense datum. Nor did they unfailingly betray the truth. Channing had bewailed that the Trinity "materialized" Divinity and, like Theodore Parker, had tested religious doctrines by the reason, ignoring as far as possible the figurative décor which muddled the ideas. What was wrong, according to Bushnell, was their attempt to "decoct the whole mass of symbol" and to carry off propositions. For religious truth was a truth not of notation but of symbol. Qualitatively different from mathematical descriptions, metaphor determined thought. The imagination had "nothing to do with ornament" but was "that power that distinguishes truths in their images, and seizes hold of images for the expression of truths." Spiritual knowledge was shaped by language. As words were the very "instruments of thought," poets were the "true metaphysicians," who would bring whatever "science of man" there would be.[28] Predating logical assent, the pattern of spiritual commitment was laid in ritual, myth, and symbol.

This singular denial that name was "Schall und Rauch" opened the way for a new semantic for theology. The problem was one not only of communication but of conception itself. Religious meanings could never be flatly given in propositions; there was "no hope" left for a science of theology. "All terms of intellect or spirit come under a wholly different law . . . from the terms of sense of the mere names of things." Yet if knowledge could be increased only by new premises, such creative insight might be won through form. The mathematical language of which Norton had dreamed could not eventuate in religious perception. Men indicated things by "exact notation," but the peculiar human power which made faith possible was the capacity to "see, in all images, the faces of truth, and take their sense, or read their meaning, when thrown up in language before the imagination."[29]

The conviction that the visible world provided a key to spiritual knowledge was not new in America, where Emerson had long chanted the eloquent power of things. Bushnell went beyond Emerson, however. For he was not content with the vocabulary of transcendental nature: though the spirit shining through things was the point of his departure, he further insisted that words, rites, and symbols could create "things" not to be found in nature. He thus proposed a symbolism which could order the world, at a time when transcendentalism, finding God impartially everywhere, threatened to dissolve all hierarchies of value. If the universe was pervaded with ubiquitous divinity, all natural metaphors uttered a monotonous testimony. The soul derived "as grand a joy from symbolizing the God-head" under the form of "a moth or a gnat as of a Lord of hosts," Emerson announced; poetically, such determined equalitarianism could issue in Whitman's cry: "scent of these arm-pits aroma finer than prayer."[30] Against this undiscriminating pantheism, Bushnell placed an ordered Christian symbolism; things were not the spiritual equivalent of every other thing, and words themselves transmitted a reality the senses could never discover.

Bushnell reinterpreted the Communion for a recalcitrant congregation through the categories of symbolic action. As innocence had been lost in the "eating of what God rejected and forbade," now grace might be apprehended in the sacrament of Communion. Christ brought the gift of divine mercy; "how more fitly" could that gift be received than by the "act of feeding upon that matter which sacramentally includes the Holy Presence expelled by our sin?" Viewing the Communion as more suited to Eastern peoples than to practical Americans, Emerson had renounced the ceremony; for "to eat bread is one thing; to love the precepts of Christ and resolve to obey them is quite another." But Bushnell, less convinced of man's ability and reasonableness, required more of religion than theorems. Christ was to be apprehended not by "thought and doctrine only" but by "some total act of faith."[31]

Since ritual, like metaphors, determined human experience, Hebrew rites were the necessary precursors of Christian understanding, not mere uncouth superstitions. As the grace of Christ was supernatural, there were "no sufficient bases of words in nature, to . . . convey it," but Jewish sacrifices, taken as "*forms* wrought into the Jewish mind, and . . . into the mind of the whole world," enabled men to grasp the meaning of Christ's history. Through animal sacrifices, the Hebrews had perceived the sacredness of the law, the horror of guilt, and the cost of forgiveness. Forms were thus prepared for the eventual Christian apprehension of Christ. Ritual provided an escape from history into the realm of

108

meaning. Form was necessary to articulate the "subjective impressions" of man, and the objectification which Hebraic customs gave to human feelings was not contingent. God had prepared Hebraic rites as forms "of art, for the representation of Christ and his work. . . . If we refuse to let [Christ] pass into this form, we have no mold of thought that can fitly represent him." For Bushnell recognized that as a mere fact of history the Crucifixion was only such a failure as made Emerson, discontent with "this great Defeat," await a more satisfactory hero, who would bring "a success to the senses as well as to the soul."[32]

Bushnell insisted that no theory could express Christ's role; one might as well attempt the "dogmatic statement" of a tragedy's meaning as to give the doctrinal equivalents for Christ's life. Apprehended through rites of sacrifice and purification, moving the human sensibility, Christ expressed God in finite form. It was a mistake to investigate the metaphysical nature of Christ. Since He had come to reveal God to man, man's only task was to experience His manifested goodness, love, and suffering. The Absolute God was hidden from the human understanding and alien to human sympathies; Christ came, as God revealed, to express the divine nature in a mode accessible to man. By His incarnation Christ expressed God's love; by His perfect obedience He taught the sanctity of the law; in his Crucifixion He revealed God's compassionate agony before the massed evil of the world. Thus he entered "into human feeling, by his incarnate charities and sufferings, to re-engage the world's love and reunite the world, as free, to the Eternal Life."[33]

In the process of accommodating Christianity to the contemporary imagination, Bushnell had transformed New England Calvinism. He explicitly attacked the sanguine trust in reason that had inspired the tomes of an Emmons or Bellamy; implicitly, he dismissed the evangelical insistence that the conviction of impotent guilt had to precede the reception of grace. His gospel did not require that the congregation face the merited wrath of God; it asked rather that they exercise "a living, ingenuous, patient, pure sensibility" before the agony and love of Christ.[34] The angry God who held men like spiders over a flaming pit was not part of the God revealed in Christ, and Bushnell refused to probe the question of Christ's intercession which had stood at the center of Calvinist hope. But he offered his public an interpretation of Christian symbolism and ritual that could order their immediate experience and their understanding of history and that could save them from a facile rationalism or an indiscriminate emotionalism.

In 1845 the *New Englander* had cheeringly remarked that the differences between Unitarianism and Congregationalism were vanishing. Modern Congregationalism required only the doctrine that Christ's incarnation and suffering were somehow essential to salvation. Such progressive orthodoxy could easily unite with Unitarianism.[35] The invitation to preach at Harvard Divinity School struck Bushnell as a providential opportunity to open the way to a more catholic and fraternal religion in New England. But *God in Christ* made too explicit the "somehow" left in amiable obscurity by the *New Englander*.

The Unitarian *Christian Examiner*, though it praised the book, feared that there was too much philosophy in it for eloquence of the "aesthetic mode" and that in the "popular" or "philosophical" part, Bushnell was not precise enough. The book was more suitable for the back country than for Boston sophistication; it offered an "admirable standpoint" for that sort of theologian who was anxious to join philosophy with appeals to the "uneducated imagination." Bushnell's conviction that forms might educate the imagination was not discussed; willing to allow the populace their symbols, Unitarians actually cared little about doctrine so long as faith was not made a "test for discipleship."[36] When Bushnell in the enthusiasm of his belief tried to argue the case with Bartol, he soon saw he had erred in taste. His next letter humbly accepted Bartol's discreet silence. "No apology was necessary for not going into an argument with me over my long, prosy letter. I did not mean to get up a paper quarrel."[37] Dr. Lowell made no move; the Hollis Chair was left vacant until 1882.

But the book released a storm among the orthodox. Reviews deplored the foggy German transcendentalism, which, according to Enoch Pond, was "befogging, bloating, and spoiling" the "clear, practical Anglo-Saxon mind." The *Christian Observatory* devoted sixty pages to denunciation, while the *Princeton Review* meticulously spelled out Bushnell's heresies. Here were Sabellianism, Docetism, Apollinarianism, Eutychianism, Pelagianism, and semi-Pelagianism.[38]

Already, groaned Enoch Pond, Bushnellites and anti-Bushnellites were appearing. The ominous sympathy of the younger clergy was conceded by the *Princeton Review.* The book had the best sale of any of Bushnell's works, and Brownson depicted its author as "one of our principal lions" in 1849. If few people were willing to champion the work explicitly, many of its doctrines crept into orthodox writings. In 1852 Edwards Park announced that the mind required truths beyond easy understanding and that Christ met the sensibility's preference for concrete truths. Though Robert Turnbull joined a hostile band of Hartford ministers against Bushnell, the *Biblical Repository* described Turnbull's *Theophany* as continuing the "semi-orthodox school of Schleiermacher, Neander, and Bushnell." To Leonard Bacon, Bushnell's doctrine came as a welcome escape from hair-splitting distinctions.[39]

111

Nonetheless, after the book appeared, Bushnell entered a period of isolation and harassment. Orthodox ministers in Hartford refused to change pulpits with him. His own ministerial association absolved him in a report which "regretted many" of his doctrines, and year after year the Fairfield West Association tried to force a trial of his heresy by the Consociation. By 1851 a majority of the associations were anxious that the original favorable verdict be reconsidered, and even loyal Noah Porter informed Bushnell that "public sentiment" required a prosecution of the case. Troubled, embittered, and frightened, Bushnell refused to permit the reopening of the question. He tried to establish his essential orthodoxy two years later in *Christ in Theology*, which pugnaciously attacked the batlike bigotry of his critics and marveled at his fortuitous agreement with the Nicene Creed.[40]

But the attack continued. Three people in Bushnell's congregation could have secured the trial he dreaded. In his ordeal Bushnell turned to his congregation and away from the outside world. He was no longer tempted to read a divine progress in history but searched for marks of election rather in exclusion and martyrdom. The suspicions of his colleagues oppressed him. "How blessed a thing it is," he wrote his wife from an Association meeting, "to retreat into God from the scowls of men, and hide in the secret of his pavilion." He saw himself standing with his church against a benighted world, and he sharply feared he might soon stand alone. In 1852, with the passion of desperation, he pleaded with his people to "stand forth in this day of Stygian darkness . . . to be the revelation of God to our blinded groping age." "O my brethren," he urgently continued, "if it should be thee that God is preparing . . . , I will refine them as silver is refined . . . and they shall call me by name and I will hear them."[41] In 1852, when a trial seemed imminent, the church withdrew from the Consocation.

In the sustained loyalty of his congregation during his estrangement, Bushnell found both grace and a judgment. If beyond the 1848 addresses he had glimpsed the prizes of a Boston pulpit or a Harvard professorship, of wider fame and public acclaim, now in his extremity his people were his sole support. Finding himself "very much cut off" from the public, he delighted in the expectation of finding God, with whom he might enter "a desert place to rest awhile. . . . I long . . . for the rest of my life, to be wholly immersed in this better element; and it is my daily prayer that God will give me . . . the gift of a private benefit . . . the usefulness of my ministry to my own flock."[42] If the imagery of the letter identified his flock with a "desert place," with refuge rather than with prophecy, his church yet seemed a "higher element."

The tensions of the minister caught between the public demand for originality and the obligations of a traditional faith were painful and unremitting. Bushnell came to accuse his insights as "temptors" distracting him from God. It was his "devil" which dealt in "invention, ingenuity, discovery."[43] An obscure antithesis between God and his own peculiar message merged with the felt division between his church and the larger public. He struggled to fix the center of his devotion with the people to whose service he had been called.

Gradually Bushnell moved closer to orthodoxy. He did not construct his later works on his semantic theories, nor did he enlarge and republish *God in Christ*, as he did *Christian Nurture*. Yet the book remains a testimony to his resolution of the tensions between ambition and faith at a turning point in his career. If as a public speaker he knew the strategic uses of metaphor, he knew also the chaos of emotional needs to which Christian forms could give coherence. His situation presses behind the pages of the book—the situation of a Hartford minister, in 1848, addressing beyond divided Congregationalists and Boston Unitarians the middle-class public of Protestant America with its quick rewards for eloquence, its dread of vulgarity, its longing and fear for the original and strange. Responsive to the time, ardent in his faith, Bushnell found an alternative to the flat common-sense moralism that threatened to reduce theology to inanity. Against an associationalist empiricism and Unitarian rationalism, he pleaded the case of the symbolic imagination.

VIII. Science and Faith

The years of harassment that followed publication of *God in Christ* were bleak and unsettling for Bushnell, now a middle-aged man. He had anticipated opening a "comprehensive vein," generous enough to satisfy all disputants. Yet his revelation had merely kindled the fury of the conservatives and the timidity of the Connecticut liberals. Neither Unitarians nor Congregationalists took up his cause. No Unitarian or Harvard advances interrupted his provincial pastorate, and he was left to attend the meetings of Congregational Associations, a suspect and controversial figure. He stood under constant threat of excommunication. Only the church he had thought of leaving stood firmly behind him.

For the first time, his letters were burdened with self-doubt and self-examination. He complained of discouragement, languor, and depression—of a "clouded mind," a "jaded and fevered state." As he read Bunyan's *Holy War*, he feared his piety had been too much of the world. He compared his religious experience with that of his wife and longed for "the same measure of fullness and peace." In 1854 he designed and ardently campaigned for a city park; yet in his dedication he felt a condemnation. He wondered that the park could so absorb his interest while as a minister he was "so feebly exercised, so little burdened" by his work. "Do we really believe that Jesus is a Saviour," he demanded of Bartol, "and that . . . he brings salvation?" The easy, occasionally glib buoyancy of his earlier years was gone; relentlessly probing his own doubts and egotism, he became "wholly dissatisfied" with himself. Seeing signs of a revival in 1854, he prayed in sudden desperation for "such a work . . . as would kill my selfishness and compel me for a time to think of nothing else."[1]

These years of self-condemnation issued in a sympathetic understanding of Pauline doctrine, which surprised Bushnell himself. For the first time, he found he could accept the severity of Calvinism. "I can see the mighty fall, the deep, unborn depravity, just as he describes it, without any sense of extravagance and without offence as against God." In his renewed sense of vocation and his growing orthodoxy, he determined to end the quarrel with Hawes and forced his doughty opponent to reconciliation by a series of public letters avowing his own strict Calvinism and irenic purposes.[2]

Yet even while these negotiations were drawing to a successful close, Bushnell found himself in "a poor bankrupt state" and complained of exhaustion and depression.[3] As his next book and all his later works were to testify, he felt increasingly that the life of faith and the tenor of the contemporary world were opposed. The cheerful expectations of his early years had dimmed. He wandered in California or settled in Hartford to some extent as one apart, elected to separateness and strangeness. For whatever price the reconciliation with Hawes exacted of Bushnell's integrity, its achievement brought the pain and resolution of a final commitment. He knew he had suffered a loss in gaining the precarious peace. With his new alliance, he sacrificed the trust of Unitarian Boston and marked himself as an irredeemable alien.

Within Hartford, Bushnell had compromised with orthodoxy; he no longer toyed with the possibility of a professor-

116

ship or another pulpit. Nonetheless, he did not relax in the search for his own peculiar message. If he stood apart, it was to reveal the eccentric insights of the prophet, saint, or heretic, not to fortify the bastions of orthodoxy. He never escaped the need for singular inspirations that the democracy demanded of the eloquent and successful. In 1853, meditating on the relationship between nature and the supernatural, he promised Bartol "a new volume or two," if he were allowed to live, "new heresies to be game for the hunters." He could not settle his ambitions at the narrow point of one congregation nor accept himself without the insights that came from his "devil" of "invention, ingenuity, discovery" or else from God.[4]

Meanwhile, ill health forced him to solitude and idleness. The years 1855 and 1856 were spent in California and Cuba. Despite the chastening of enmities and sickness, however, a resilient faith in himself and his work made him hold tenaciously to active life. He rebelled against illness because it threatened his projected book on *Nature and the Supernatural*. "It costs me a great trial to let go, if I must, before I have done that which I have been regarding as the main work and principal meaning of my life."[5]

Separated from his church, he pictured himself in his "prophet's chamber," where he pondered whether he had not made the "modern" error of living too much in the world. Prophet-like, he came to rely on the successive visions that would guarantee his religious fidelity and his originality. He did not turn to religious tradition in the Bible or in theology but looked for new revelations. As he worked on *Nature and the Supernatural*, he considered the problem of continuing inspiration. Again and again, with untiring concern, he reverted to the issue, insisting that God would continue to speak directly to men. "There is no evidence whatever," he wrote, "that we are required to be less inspired, or in a lower sense, or that we are farther shut away from God and the Word of the Lord, than they were in former ages." Certain men in every age, he concluded, had been called to reveal new divine truths; such men had a vocation to be prophets as others had to be "shoemakers or bankers."[6] Cut off from worldly expectations, Bushnell had found his calling.

He had long ago eschewed comprehensive systems of divinity. Bushnell prided himself on his progress in understanding and faith, and when faced with new illuminations he as readily dropped his own past as he had dropped New England theological traditions. *God in Christ* completed, Bushnell sought a knowledge of God beyond forms; in 1852, he joyfully wrote his wife that he had at last experienced God beyond all "physical images and measures" and beyond the reach of "even the imagination."[7]

Bushnell thought in terms of the successive messages of his books. Emphasis, approach, and concepts changed. Published in 1858, *Nature and the Supernatural* did not revive the semantic problems of *God in Christ* but centered on the cosmological necessity of redemption by Christ. The new volume made the supernatural powers of the will crucial. Yet two years later Bushnell republished *Christian Nurture* with its implication that a Christian will could be shaped within the family. Though he enlarged the book to include more detailed advice on child care, Bushnell still described the molding of the will by habit and failed to clarify the relation of Christ to the grace of education.

But it was the new book, with its promise of holding the "principal meaning" of his life, which absorbed him. *Nature and the Supernatural* betrayed new anxieties. For the first time, one of Bushnell's major works expressed sharp alienation. The sense of an imperiled Christianity ran through its pages as an insistent and dissonant motif. Bushnell no longer exulted in the certain historical progress he had detected in 1843 when an "appeal to truth and reason" seemed enough to end evil. Rather, faith was hemmed in by enemies—science, Fourierism, magnetism, phrenology, Biblical criticism, Unitarianism, and transcendentalism. The Christian world was moving toward the "vanishing point of faith." Preaching was impotent; religious experience was meager and suspect; the topic of religion in private conversation was avoided. In 1847 Bushnell had jubilantly noted that the Protestant Alliance was harnessing religion to the age; now he saw only disjunction between the victorious spirit of the times and the meaning of religion. Christian experience required some "broad and palpable line of suffering," which cut it off from the world. Without the expense of such pain, the church would sink into an easy humanitarianism, bringing finally "some terrible reaction, some war of Gog and Magog, that shall empty the church from vessel to vessel."[8]

The book testified to a new estrangement from the learned, who fecklessly followed every fad. If Christ had had to rely on the intellectuals, He would "scarcely [have] left a follower." But the mass of people more responsibly guarded the deposit of faith. "They testify to one faith, and live one common life of grace, in all ages."[9]

In conception Bushnell's new project recalled the patient systems of divinity of an earlier era. Taylor would have been gratified by its far-flung dimensions. The scale was the history of the world; the purpose, the justification of God's government; the method, the explication of an orderly system. As Bartol was to lament, the book was, fatally, a "scheme."[10]

Nonetheless, Nature and the Supernatural was directed to the enlightened American public which was being beguiled by science and transcendentalism. During the 1840's and 1850's, an audience with new information and perspectives had emerged, and in *Nature and the Supernatural* Bushnell addressed himself to a public less concerned with the imagination and the heart than with geology, progress, and reason.

All three of the public's new interests undermined inherited faith: geology contradicted the Mosaic account of creation and suggested to some that organic life might have developed slowly from the lowest forms up to man; technological progress fostered human pride and challenged the Christian pattern of history; finally, transcendentalism, by scoffing at miracles, enthusing over human progress, and denying man's need of intercession, seemed to sum up the time's heresies and offer the public a faith adapted to its credulity. Bushnell set himself the task of answering these infidelities by a reformulation of Christian divinity.

"From the first moment . . . of modern science," *Nature and the Supernatural* announced, with more temerity than it was to sustain, "it has been clear that Christianity must ultimately come into a grand issue of life and death with it."[11] For science threatened to make myths of miracles and a science of religion. Bushnell knew the long uneasy altercations between scientific discoveries and orthodox convictions. He had witnessed religion's reluctant, compromised retreats before an attentive public, which seemed more excited by science than by imperiled faith. There was, and had long been, adequate cause for alarm.

Orthodox nervousness had begun with the collision between geology and the Mosaic account of creation. Initially, the New England ministry treated geological investigations with determined aloofness. Later, indignation at the new mode of testing revelation issued in a series of denunciations. The conflict was patent; the only question was what was to be done. "Let it be a question, whether Moses has taught wrongly or rightly," Moses Stuart pleaded in 1836, "but it can never be a question with philologists whether modern science is to be the first judge of what an ancient writing means."[12]

But neither indifference nor hostility nor philology could withstand the fascination of science. By mid-century Hitchcock was warning that in case of apparent conflict the "intelligent man" would probably side with science, and the *Princeton Review* testified that thousands of people thought science rested on a firmer basis than the Bible. If the Bible were opposed to science, James Dana announced, the younger generation would "scout" the Bible.[13]

The people determinedly sought out the unsettling discoveries of science. In 1834 Silliman gave a popular series of geological lectures in Hartford; speaking in Boston, he was flattered by large audiences and the calling cards of Boston's elite. Science, which relied not on abstractions but on "skeletons, trees, and stones," dominated people's imaginations, and in 1858 the *Atlantic Monthly* contrasted the "little heeded lyre of theology" with the "mighty organ of modern science."[14]

In the face of such popular enthusiasm, religion had little recourse. By 1849 the *Bibliotheca Sacra* was urging the minister to study science, for only by natural knowledge could he impress "practical men" who usually assumed that theologians had no common sense. By mid-century, religious periodicals devoted much of their space to the impact of science on religion. Most writers energetically accommodated the new learning by the generous expansion of doctrine; yet even the hospitable were frightened at times. In 1851 the *New Englander*, which had long championed science, abruptly betrayed the strains beneath its cheery conciliations. "Where is science tending? What can be thrown out to check her?"[15]

This new information forced a series of strategic retreats upon those who hoped for serene adjustment. As no one

121

could settle on a line of defense, believers squabbled over what was dispensable to faith. At Amherst, Hitchcock crammed all geologic time into the interval between the "beginning" and the first day and explained that sudden devastation had made the earth "waste and void" just before the creation of the first day; but the *Bibliotheca Sacra* insisted that geology proved that nature's progress had been continuous, without any such reversion to chaos. Though the *Bibliotheca Sacra* doubted that an ark 450 by 75 by 45 feet could hold "1,658 species of birds, 642 species of reptiles and tortoises, and 120,000 species of insects," the *Princeton Review* insisted that unless the flood was universal, the Bible was not the Word of God.[16]

But the primary menace of science was not the evidence which upset Biblical history. Its very method of discovering, recognizing, and assessing truth challenged the idea of revelation. A new mode of conviction was being established. In the early days, Silliman had feared that laymen would never understand the geologists' certainty that rock layers could not have been constructed by divine fiat, but it was soon evident that his fears had been misplaced. By the 1850's only an articulate but neglected minority remained to mourn the changed locus of faith. The Bible emerged as a feebler, more fragmentary revelation. "If the earth as a whole is not a trustworthy document, there can be no reliance on particles of its substance made into a book," the *Bibliotheca Sacra* brusquely announced. With the guardians of orthodoxy so intoxicated, Emerson could freely rejoice that "geology has initiated us into the secularity of nature and taught us to dismiss our dame school measures, and exchange our Mosaic and Ptolemaic schemes for her large style."[17]

When Bushnell set about preparing lectures on "Nature and the Supernatural," he girded himself, as always, to meet the contemporary mind. He had studied under Silliman and conversed with Dana; he had read Miller, Agassiz, and John Pye Smith, and he was ready to concede much. Geology had revealed, and theology had to take account of, a revised history of the universe. Bushnell declined to juggle with the dimensions of the Ark or to puzzle over the growth of plants before the creation of the sun: he was anxious rather to integrate the total sweep of the new history within the framework of Christian theology. His strategy was inherited from New Haven; unlike students of Andover's Stuart, he had no substantial investment in Biblical exegesis, and in the crisis his disengagement proved serviceable. *Nature and the Supernatural* disregarded particulars in the attempt to sustain the Christian drama within the time spans of geology.

Bushnell borrowed his method from science, presenting his doctrine as a hypothesis to be judged by its adequacy to experience. He pretended to no mathematical certainty but urged that his theory "like every hypothesis that gathers in, accommodates, and assimilates, all the facts of the subject," should be accepted as true.[18]

In some ways geological findings fitted in with Calvinist presuppositions. Rock layers and fossils left room for discrete act of creation, which corresponded to the orthodox vision of God. As Unitarians and transcendentalists increasingly entertained the thesis that all organisms had progressively developed from each other, Congregationalists clung the more feverishly to geological evidences.

The "development hypothesis" seemed far more subversive than geology to many orthodox men. Yet by 1849 Emerson appended his vision of spiraling animal evolution to his essay on "Nature," and the *Christian Examiner* exultantly announced in 1853 that, since progress ruled all life, man's few, diminishing faults would eventually be abolished. Christ, too, was fitted in the forward rush of Nature. As Nature continually improved her own "productions," His

123

coming was not a startling event. The sole oddity was that He should have arrived so soon.[19]

Bushnell protested against this linear view of progress which was capturing the public imagination, and he called upon geological evidence to support the Christian pattern of history. The new learning diverted men's thoughts from the question of personal conversion. The revelation of God in the strange world of geology and the justifiability of His peculiar ways engrossed the attention of believers. Not haggling over Biblical exegesis, Bushnell reminded readers of the uneven creation geology recorded: the venomous, wriggling serpent that shared the earth with "stately mammalia," the "fiery cataclysms" that interrupted growth. In disproof of the steady ascent of organic life, he pointed to the recent and deformed halibut with its "twisted mouth," "Cyclopian eye," "asymmetrical jaws." Yet man had joined this mixed creation, and *Nature and the Supernatural* praised geology for having revealed the "very times and places where the hand of God was inserted into the world."[20]

Yet the threat of the new sciences reached beyond new evidence, new temporal sequences, and new modes of proof. The blithe certainty of man's self-impelled progress endangered the Christian view of man more fundamentally than fossil remains did. Bushnell had to cope with the flattering image of man the creator which scientific and technical achievements were engraving on the consciousness of the time. "Worship," according to Thomas King, was the only word "deep enough to express the Anglo-Saxon relation to the mechanical powers and arts." Quickened expectations attended a new type of hero; according to the Commissioner of Patents, only inventors could solve the "great problems of existence."[21]

With such onerous opportunities, man assumed a new relation to the creation and the Creator. The issue of existence lay less between God and man than between man and nature. The struggle had been close, but its eventual outcome was happily clear. The Patent Commissioner, viewing the world as a "workshop," reversed the concept of man's fall. "Fire gives us what Eden had not. If a flaming sword drove one man out, the knowledge of flame has put within the reach of all men blessings unknown there." Bushnell shared the common enthusiasm. Giving man power to "recompose and re-create the world," science made gods of men.[22]

Like the "development hypothesis," technical progress suggested a linear view of history. For the *Christian Examiner*, the crucial point of history was not Christ but the investigations of Aristotle, with which man began his ascent from the "state of nature into a state of spiritual light and grace." *Nature and the Supernatural* marveled at the "grand commercial apostleship of steam and telegraph" which prepared for the sovereignty of Christian ideas.[23] Geology extended the vision of the past, and science invited fantasies on the future, but neither was adjusted for focus on thirty-three remote years in human history.

In mid-century the outlines and method of science remained so fuzzy that its threat merged for orthodox thinkers with that of transcendentalism. To Bushnell, both were guilty of naturalism, and he attacked both with the same weapons. Like geology, transcendentalism tended to turn the Bible into myth; in addition, it asserted that the Reason did not need myth, for the mind could directly confront the Truth. Transcendentalism heightened scientific disinterest in the miraculous into disdain. Parker derided Christ's miracles as inferior to those of Vishnu and explained them as the product of a benighted era. Glorifying man, denying that he needed intercession, transcendentalism answered the popular enthusiasm for humanity's progress.

Religious fear and controversy in the Northeast centered

in the transcendentalism which, according to the *New Englander*, was converting many of the "most gifted men of the day." Within Boston, as outside of it, Theodore Parker became the occasion of bitter debate. Transcendentalism proved so formidable a foe that Unitarian Andrews Norton published a Presbyterian exposé of the transcendentalists' ignorance of German thought. "What," Bushnell asked the reticent Bartol, was Boston—"Boston above all"—saying of *Nature and the Supernatural?*[24]

In his critique of transcendentalism, as in his response to geology and technology, Bushnell did not entirely dismiss the new theories but took over the ideas he found true. He was already committed to intuitive knowledge, which Congregationalist and Presbyterian orthodoxy ridiculed, and he, like Parker, habitually disparaged theologies. Like Parker, he was anxious to prove that inspiration was still possible and to speak to the large audiences, the "elegant and the young," who crowded transcendentalist lectures.[25] Accordingly, his book appropriated many of Parker's contentions and put them in the service of orthodoxy. Bushnell refused to accept the idea that the Christian God was arbitrary or irrational in dispensing favors; he looked forward to the time when men would be able to "connect more certainly, and more in the manner of science, with the resources of God." He promised that eventually a "rational, scientific . . . ingrafting" of grace would be possible, as religious knowledge increased.[26]

But, though Bushnell, like the transcendentalists, exploited the optimism created by science, he refused to accept the linear progress promised by technology and described by transcendentalists and Unitarians. He persistently denied that redemption was possible without a cleavage in history and an intervening grace. Whatever the human powers, man lived in alienation from God, the easy prey of a corrupted will and an evil society. The successful conclusion of all reform movements would be the "greatest imaginable misfortune" so long as the soul remained separate from God.[27]

Bushnell started with man, not with nature. To insure man's crucial isolation from other organisms, he turned to Coleridge's distinction between powers and things. As a power, man was free. Unlike the rest of nature, he was not determined by "things" but controlled his own moral destiny. Morally, though his obligations were decreed by the known law of right, he was free to sin, and because the will had chosen evil instead of good, he was a damned and lost being. His own sinful election stood at the center of his history.

Still, Bushnell did not follow Coleridge's doctrine of the transcendent evil of the will; he proved man's freedom by pointing to the human power to master nature, and he explained human sin as the inevitable result of curiosity. Man as inventor and experimenter, as efficient cause, held his imagination. Adam, the archetype of mankind, was not so much corrupt as in a "condition privative" of virtue. Though he knew the law, he had also to discover the meaning of right and wrong through experience.

Schooled in empiricism, Bushnell could not conceive of Coleridge's realm of Reason, where commands were valid because they transcended experienced sensations and emotions. For Bushnell, no moral idea was finally established until experience had drilled man into knowledge of its truth. The world was the training ground for moral agency, since even to be a "power" man needed to have experienced both a fall and a redemption. Experience thus served to fortify the will, and even the fall had its beneficence. Adam had been lost by his very innocence; only the "new man," exercised and trained in the fallen world, would achieve, with grace, an impregnable virtue.

127

Bushnell could not conceive of the Christian dilemma save as the issue of man's attainment of righteousness; the central drama of his book was not the need for justification, which had troubled Augustine and Luther, but man's quest for a "truly divine virtue," "where the good is followed because it is good, and right because it is right, God because He is God." Salvation did not depend upon the commutation of God's wrath but upon a goodness man could not achieve alone. Such redeeming virtue was a new state, "a right disposedness, whence new action may flow." It was a psychological condition of spontaneous rectitude, in which righteousness was the play of the soul.[28]

However exorbitant Bushnell's ambitions for man, he nonetheless maintained that the fall could not be redeemed through nature or experience, and he supported his orthodoxy with geological evidence which Parker and Emerson for the most part ignored and which seemed to the time a testament of horrors. The nature in which Parker had deciphered bounding, universal joy was marked for Bushnell by death, catastrophe, and degradation. Proving that death of animals had predated the fall, geology revealed a world damned from the first in the sight of God. The extinction of innumerable species was token of eternal condemnation. To Emerson, Nature was "a fixed point whereby we may measure our departure. . . . We are as much strangers in Nature, as we are aliens from God." But Bushnell saw in nature the "deformity, jargon, death," which would scourge man's sinfulness and was suited to his depravity.[29]

The new science was thus made to serve the Christian conviction that evil was central in the world. Yet the disorder of nature was not endemic, for the source of the corruption which encompassed life was a human apostasy. The irreparable choice of evil by the will, enacted in time and foreseen in eternity, initiated the shock that turned nature into "unnature"—a "whole creation groaning and travailling in pain."[30] Its order had been hurled into chaos by man as "power" when he sinfully chose experience over the obligations of the law. The causes and effects of "things" had been disjointed by sin, and no restoration was possible within the realm of nature, fallen with man.

The agony of natural existence did indeed serve God's discipline. Yet, though the mechanism of retributive justice might beat man into contrite recognition of his guilt and even into legal obedience, it could not redeem. Legal morality might be achieved, but obedience based on fear or self-interest remained bondage. All nature's severe training issued only in hypocrisy.

Nor was salvation accessible through self-reliance. Man could not hope, as Emerson had beguilingly suggested, to cut himself from the interwoven corruptions of society and find redemption in the far reaches of the individual consciousness. The individual was trapped by the human past and molded by a sinful society; powerless, the infant entered an organic order that presided over his weakness and determined his character. Emerson's vision of the willed, lonely capture of individual liberty was a fantasy. "Society is, in all its vast complications, an appointment—we can not escape it."[31]

The individual was so possessed by his inherited depravity that in fact his dependence on society was a blessing. The apparent curse of social corruption saved him from the bleaker horror of atomic independence. By the weakness of infancy and the institution of the family, man was set apart from the brutality of nature to be nurtured in the forms of civilization. If these were not the forms of "holy virtue," they were closer to it than the wild nature of geology or the ruthlessness of unchecked individualism. "The civil law is ... a restraint on development.... It forbids men to unfold

themselves freely, in their base passions and criminal insti-
gations."[32] Left to himself, the individual would find life
nasty, brutish, short; instead, he was trained in the discipline
of the law and within the family came to know love.

The focal point of *Nature and the Supernatural*, however,
was not the family, which was part of the fallen world. Salvation could come only through the piercing of history and
nature by the divine. In spite of his transcendent will, man
could not save himself, for the order of nature had been
unhinged by his initial choice. Though, impelled by the
sanctions of the law and nature, he might self-interestedly
do the right, his acts were worthless without the transformed status of the soul which was virtue.

All hope of regeneration depended upon God. "Christianity is . . . a power out of nature and above, descending
into it; a historically supernatural movement on the world,
that is visibly entered into it."[33] Christ was the unique agent
of salvation, whom no spiraling of nature could have produced and without whose presence man could never have
escaped the bondage of society or his own corruption.

Bushnell did not concern himself with the relation of
Christ to Old Testament prophecy, nor did he base his case
for Christ's divinity upon the miracles. Instead, he pictured
the man he found in the Bible, who challenged human society and common sense. Christ's life subverted human standards. He invested himself with innocence, though innocence
was commonly derided as a feeble thing; He consorted with
the vile, the outcast, the derelict. Worst of all by the standards of reason, He made such exorbitant claims about his
person that He could only have been a madman if he were
not God.

Yet this odd intruder upon world history was its Savior.
The Christ of Mark Hopkins "in his piety, in his benevolence and other virtues, in the refinement and delicacy of

his character" could serve as a "suitable" model for gentle-
men, and the *Christian Examiner* found it impossible to distinguish the "voice of nature" from that of Christ. But
Bushnell's Christ stood beyond the pale of social decorum
and subverted nature. No "natural evidences" could lead
men to imagine so unconventional and eccentric a figure.
The procedures of faith were peculiar. "Christ came into the
world to bestow himself. . . . He is a new premise, that could
not be reasoned, but must first *be*, and then can be received
only by faith."[34]
    The concept was hazardous, not least so for Bushnell him-
self. It opened the possibility that Christianity had nothing
to do with science, and if so, the entire framework of *Nature
and the Supernatural* might collapse. Prudently, the book
left the structural strains obscure, but in *Sermons for the
New Life*, published the same year, Bushnell set forth the
alien and exorbitant demands of faith. It was futile, he had
decided, to accumulate arguments and evidence. Unlike
scientific belief, faith was won by a commitment that defied
evidences and refused to weigh probabilities. It initiated in
a voluntary assent, which natural evidences could not justify
or create. Knowledge was achieved only after a perilous act
of trust. Proof came later, when proof was no longer needed.
Initially, "one being, a sinner, commits himself to another
being, a Saviour."[35] Forerunning data, defying likelihood,
faith demanded the risk of a prior consent.
    With *Nature and the Supernatural* Bushnell entered a new
field, seeking, as Dwight and Taylor had done earlier, to
rationalize man's history and experience within a Christian
framework. Attempting to re-establish the Christian view of
man, he called upon the testimony of science and made man
as creator and inventor the protagonist of the human drama.
Yet he challenged contemporary humanism, even as he took
account of it. He no longer, he wrote, longed to be thought

131

a "liberal."[36] With his final resolution to remain a Hartford preacher, he had moved this much closer to Connecticut theology and orthodox Christianity. He had spoken of a fallen world and a corrupted humanity, of the foolishness of atomic individualism. He refused to see the history of the world as the steady ascension to nineteenth-century virtue, and he restricted human hope to a brief, remote break in history.

Reviews of the book were lengthy, ponderous, and uninspired. Though Bartol in the *Christian Examiner* dubbed it the "chief theological work of its time" the general commendations, weighted with quotations, everywhere thudded somewhat dutifully. The *New Englander* chiefly remarked that the book had established what the *New Englander* had never doubted—the moral agency of man. However appropriate to science, in religion the ratiocinative method was out of date. Bartol protested, that so argumentative a treatise was alien to "the Bible and . . . Nature." Such unremitting rationality could veer in only one direction; clearly, it led the author to the edge of "absurdity." As readers of the *Christian Examiner* well knew, even to have produced the "chief theological work of its time" was a dubious investment of energy. More specifically, Bartol protested that to consider man to be evil was a libel on God. All in all, the volume struck him as "supernaturalism run mad."[37]

Bushnell had waited impatiently for notices of his book. But when reaction finally came, he felt let down, even "persecuted." "Almost everything said on one side is thrown back on the other, and I am pelted all round," he complained to Bartol. Had all his research and planning produced nothing but confusion? There were discouraging portents. No school or group was taking up his ideas; no publication fostered his gospel, though any of these, he was sure, would have strengthened his cause. The public had been given the "main work" and "principal meaning" of his life and had received the gift with cavils and studied praise. He was forced to conclude that his time had "not yet come" and would not, "till after I am gone." Yet he clung to faith in his work. His health became so poor that he was unable to preach, but by New Year's Day of 1859 he was dreaming of a vague though vast new program. If he had no church and an uncertain public, if he had known only equivocal successes, a stubborn, restless ardor held him to his chosen vocation. "I think the day is at hand when something can be done for a better conception of the work of Christ. Here is the great field left that I wait for grace and health to occupy."[38]

IX. The Law of Sacrifice

The commotion following *God in Christ* was not repeated with *Nature and the Supernatural*. If reviewers recommended the book, they lavished more spontaneous enthusiasm on *Sermons for the New Life*, published the same year. Rejoicing that sermons at last were "popular and successful" literary "wares," the *New Englander* was so delighted that it compared Bushnell to Henry Ward Beecher. Though the reviewer hinted Bushnell might be too logical and thorough for total enjoyment, he assured the indolent that the exertion required for reading Bushnell would be rewarded by new insights.[1]

No reviewer of *Nature and the Supernatural* mentioned the promise of the pages where Bushnell set for himself his final major task—"the great field left that I wait for grace and health to occupy." He proposed to offer a treatise on "the laws of God's Supernatural kingdom," convinced that "no other contribution to the truth of Christ is so much needed, or promises results of so great moment." By 1861, he had a rough outline of the ambitious project, in which he hoped to set forth the meaning of the atonement. The plan was massive, in the tradition of New England divinity; he would require two volumes. The first would deal with the law of sacrifice as fulfilled in Christ; the second with its realization in believers. If the public had a yen for laws, what laws could be of more crucial consequence? Logic was on Bushnell's side, but by the time he published a second volume, he included an apologia to remind the public of the strength of his case. "Let us count our salvation," he pleaded, "a matter high enough and rich enough to be studied, searched out, nicely discriminated."[2]

As he took up the work, he met few interruptions save the constant pain and discomforts of sickness. He had been forced to resign his pastorate in 1859 because of his poor health, and the church gave him ten thousand dollars when he left. An adequate income secure, his position no longer susceptible to drastic change, Bushnell could turn to his appointed task without the distraction of mixed ambitions. "This . . . is going now to be our lot from this time forward," he wrote his wife in 1861, "a stay in old Hartford, and no more experiments, letting the clock run down as it will." He wrote from the isolation of his independence. For the first time, a large-scale enterprise failed to reflect contemporary concerns. But a curious exaltation seized Bushnell as he bent to his chosen work. "I don't know what I have done that God should bless me so, in giving me such a call, and work, and subject, and leisure, and means, at the closing of my days, that I may fill up my measure."[3]

Increasingly, Bushnell assumed, to others and to himself, the lineaments of prophet and seer. When he spoke, he seemed to descend from a privileged seclusion. Listening to the gaunt and aging man, men recalled the prophets of the Old Testament. "Truth lay between him and God, not between him and the Church"; he seemed to have come to deliver the vision he had been permitted "on the Mount."[4]

He had reached the time of life commonly given over to new editions and memoirs, but he could not let go. Still possessed by some fierce, insatiable ambition, he refused to consider his work done. Cut off from practical goals, he turned

135

again and again to the faith that he still had a call, that God was still granting him new insights and a crucial message.[5]

Yet his activity issued from a costly resignation. If he wrote feverishly, he wrote with chastened expectations. He had come to distinguish between his own conviction and the mere "eidolon of it which words could convey," and though he continued to work for communication, he was resigned to the idea that communication involved falsification. He lived by the inspirations of his solitude, reconciled to spiritual separation from his audience. Convinced of the truth of the *Vicarious Sacrifice*, he doubted only the adequacy of his expression. Listeners at this time found his delivery like "a solitary meditation on his absorbing theme."[6]

The Civil War had seemed a vindication of his role. It figured in his thought as the culmination of the atomistic political theory which he had earlier condemned and which the nation had had to expiate in blood and suffering. As prophet he had been justified; now he must once again take on the prophet's obligation to interpret, sustain, and direct the nation, which had become a conscious moral entity.

Events had favored his reassertion of the ministry's political prerogatives, for at last, anxious for military and moral unity, the public required leadership of the clergy. Furthermore, the situation no longer forced a choice between the righteous emancipation of slaves or a pious acquiescence in the status quo. As the war joined the causes of the established government and the abolition of slavery, the uncomfortable alternatives between which Bushnell's political theory had oscillated were obliterated. At last, Christian duty pointed in only one direction.

Bushnell welcomed his double enfranchisement. He spoke repeatedly in Hartford and once in Yale Chapel upon the war. By language and analogies he set the war within the Hebraic-Christian tradition. Perceiving the conflict through

Christian categories, he discovered in it condemnation and atonement. "We have, at last, come to the point where only blood . . . can resanctify what we have so loosely held and so badly desecrated."[7] Interpreted through Christian sacrifice and redemption, the war became for Bushnell a decisive, even a final, moment of America's history, lifting the nation forever beyond secularism. For men of the next generation like Gladden and Abbott, the Civil War would be the first blow in the long battle for social perfection; to Bushnell, it revealed the eternal necessity for tragedy and bloodshed and pointed away from history to Christ's eternal sacrifice.

America had been transformed. The nation could no longer accept lightly the union it had purchased in pain, and the people could righteously participate in a government that had removed the sin of slavery. The promise of the times stretched toward an idyllic perfection, until perhaps government itself might disappear "in the freedom of a righteousness consummated in God."[8] Unlike the next generation of liberal ministers, Bushnell believed the way to the millennial society to be primarily blocked by individual, not by social, sin. The war had won the nation's rectitude; men should now be free to turn their thoughts to their own salvation. Thus ordered by his faith, the Civil War did not deflect but reinforced Bushnell's dedication to the task of delineating the "laws of the supernatural."

He had already assigned the world of science and history to its place in the Christian cosmogony; now he could devote himself to that higher economy where the laws of "the heart" obtained. In the emancipation of these later years, Bushnell thus returned to the familiar realm of the romantic sensibility, and his final major volume followed the bent of his conversion experience. Once again he was focusing upon the emotion of the Christian drama, and he sought the "poetry" of the occasion.[9] Yet, though *Vicarious Sacrifice* restated many doctrines of *God in Christ*, new discriminations had entered Bushnell's thought.

Like his favorite readings, Bushnell's personal experience gathered his energies around the dilemma of Christian love. In his long struggle to commute the years of persecution and the bristling combativeness of his own temperament into a Christian temper, he had increasingly studied the uses and requirements of pain. In the chastened isolation, which, he felt, had brought him close to God, the question of religious knowledge had come to seem less crucial than the sacrificial suffering that stood at the center of Christianity. In this sacrifice he was finding strange implications. Though he had long shared the common belief that the soul intuitively knew the right and that Christianity could readily be grasped by the untutored mind, at the end of his life he decided that missionary teaching was difficult, even impossible. For, though the heathen might easily apprehend a God of love, they would balk at the singular doctrine that God would seek after a corrupt humanity. "To believe that he comes after us through painstaking and sorrow would be very far off—ah, it is impossible."[10]

In this perception of Christianity he felt that he had reached the climax of his religious experiences. "Now I lay hold of and appropriate the fact of God's vicarious character in goodness, and of mine to be accomplished in Christ as a follower."[11] The conviction measured the troubled, alienated years since *God in Christ*. Now it had become clear that Christian existence could not be adequately apprehended by the symbolic imagination; at the center of Christianity stood the practical obligation of Christ's exorbitant love and mysterious sacrifice. Caught by this strange vision, Bushnell contrasted the aesthetic and Christian emotions, which the "refined" contemporary Protestantism and his own *God in Christ* had so narrowly joined. Aesthetic love required "only a natural capacity of sentiment" and spontaneously issued from the full heart. But Christian love, which began with "the loss of all things," broke into the heart only when it was destitute.

Bushnell's absorption in the love behind the atonement estranged him from his theological traditions and from America's immediate enthusiasms. The New England theology had not centered on the person or the sacrifice of Christ. From the time of Edwards' ecstatic consent to "Being in General," religious expectation had sought rather a selfless surrender to the divine order. Under Hopkins and his disciples, the test of regeneration had been the willing acceptance of personal damnation, if such damnation contributed to the fullness of God's glory. Such lines of aspiration could not easily converge on the sacrifice of Christ. As it was drawn in testimonials in the *Connecticut Evangelical Magazine*, the pattern of nineteenth-century conversions identified penance with the sinner's recognition of his own hostility to a limited atonement, and it deciphered regeneration in the penitent's blissful acceptance of the divine order.

True, the multiplication of theological speculation that followed Edwards issued in New England's peculiar contribution to theology: the moral government theory of the atonement. Yet, though it dealt with Christ's work, this New England "improvement" centered the experience of regeneration at a far remove from Christ's work. For according to the New England school, Christ had died to make divine forgiveness consistent with the moral law which man had desecrated; his atonement made it possible for God to forgive men honorably but "had no bearing on our positive reward." The sacrifice of Christ was irrelevant to the salvation of the individual sinner. "God grants regenerating grace to whom he pleases," Emmons explained, "as an act of mere sovereignty, without any particular respect to the death or

139

atonement of Christ." Under such a dispensation, the preacher should perceive that his task was to show sinners God's
hate rather than His love, Emmons urged.[12]

Though the more strategic Calvinism of Taylor avoided
Emmons' ferocity, he too failed to focus on the work of
Christ. Like his predecessors, he could conceive no shorter
way to religious experience than through knowledge of the
total structure of God's moral government. Though it was
left to Unitarians and transcendentalists to suggest that
Christ's sacrifice was supererogatory, Connecticut orthodoxy
found it equally superfluous for the central business of revivals. Taylor, Beecher, and their followers confronted sinners with the choice of moral obedience or damnation,
knowing that every man would recognize the rule of right
he might savingly follow. For every sinner was graced with
the moral insights of common sense.

At another pole of American faith, where transcendentalists reigned, the proofs of the benevolent structure of God's
government were not searched out with the passionate, voluminous logic of back-country professors. Yet transcendentalists were no more content than Edwards, Hopkins, or
Taylor with a partial assault upon totality. "No bar or wall
in the soul," wrote Emerson, shut man from God. "The soul
gives itself, alone, original, and pure, to the Lonely, Original,
and Pure, who, on that condition, gladly inhabits, leads, and
speaks through it."[13] If the necessary discipline was severe,
still the soul could receive and apprehend that alien energy,
which had its center everywhere and which had no circum-
ference. Transcendentalists, like the Congregationalists they
deplored, sought the revelation of the whole and disdained a
mediated vision.

In 1849 Bushnell had set forth the role of Christ in religious perception; now he discovered in Christ's work the
unique Christian imperative. If he found little encourage-

ment for his Christology in his immediate America, he could comfort himself with the thought that not he but his culture was playing the provincial. In Germany Schleiermacher had initiated a new concern with Christ, and in England Frederick Maurice was centering the Gospel in Christ's sacrifice. Bushnell could find in Maurice's books, with which he had stocked his library, the central figure of a suffering God in a condemned world. Though he never shared Maurice's interest in the Judaic-Christian dispensation, Bushnell found in *The Doctrine of Sacrifice* the idea that only God's sacrificial descent could redeem a corrupt world and turn the human spirit from its self-will and isolation. By this fellowship of conviction, Bushnell was saved from total eccentric isolation and from what he dreaded more: from identification with the long-winded, outmoded orthodoxy of rural Connecticut.

For, within America, Bushnell's harsh picture of the world was singular. Unitarians had basked in a genteel and kindly universe; later, transcendentalists had preached the accessible beatitude of union with the Infinite; most recently, young radicals were glorying in the evolutionary sequences of the natural world. Yet, though Emerson promised that the unmediated reception of nature might bring absolution, the universe seemed to Bushnell to be so antagonistic to God that it baffled any such ecstasy of surrender. No human beatitude could be won without the intervening grace of God. Nor could Bushnell trace the history of redemption in the upward surge of evolutionary progress. The universe was "essentially tragic. With a fall and an overspreading curse at the beginning, and a cross in the middle, and a glory and shame at the end."[14]

As Bushnell settled down to isolation and as he accepted his personal communion with God, his conviction of disparity between God and the world intensified. He was ready to agree in 1866 that the story of the fall might be myth, not describing but giving form and significance to historical fact; but he insisted that experience revealed that man was fallen and the world corrupt. Occasionally he saw a radical disjunction between God and His creation. The perception, so strange to his century, opened for his amazement the nature of divine love. The Christian God could only be known through His inexplicable sacrifice of Himself for an "accursed thing."[15]

The antithesis between creature and Creator promised to undermine the common-sense rationalism upon which Taylor's theology had been built. In these later years Bushnell's hostility to Taylor re-emerged in full force, giving his speculations a welcome target. He volubly assaulted the moral-government theory, repeating that a just God could not vindicate the moral law through the sufferings of innocence. Taylor's governmental analogies, which had met the enthusiasms of fledgling republicans, failed to satisfy the moral absolutism of the romantic temper. For Bushnell, as for Emerson and Thoreau, the highest ethical order transcended and might even subvert political obligations. God's intrinsic being, grace, and faith, Bushnell asserted, could never be apprehended under political analogies.

True, man's fall initiated the penal sequences of the natural order, which were the discipline of moral government. But grace and faith annulled the political bond, restoring man to a communion with God which obliterated all question of retributions and rewards. Love and mercy constituted the essential, immediate nature of God; justice and punishment were governmental devices necessitated by man's fall. As in the beginning God had been united to innocent man, so through the atonement He surpassed governmental strategies and restored the possibility of a union of perfect love. Once again man and God could meet in a free moral bond that made the pleasure-pain calculus of God's common government superfluous. With grace, man renewed his relationship with the intrinsic Godhead and by this recovery achieved a Christian liberty.

The law at the center of existence was not political but sentimental; it was the law of love. A necesssity in the divine nature, crossed by the evil and need of a fallen world, issued in sacrifice. For there was "a Gethsemane hid in all love," and Christ's agony expressed the essential sorrow of passion. "By that sign it was that God's love broke into the world, and Christianity was born."[16]

Like Taylor, Bushnell glimpsed in God's transcendence a Being whose reliable morality spared man both perplexity and dread, although new tensions played through Bushnell's dialectic. He claimed that the love behind the atonement was the clear, universal law of love; yet he spoke of God's compassion "breaking" upon the world and of the revelation brought by Christ. He required an odd double vision of human intuition, by which man was at once to understand the orderly processes of good moral government and at the same time to apprehend the politically subversive law of virtue which enjoined an unsettling love. Gladly as Bushnell might have rested in these ambiguities, no such serene haziness was to be permitted him. But the challenge came later, and from a more sophisticated quarter than Connecticut: from the redoubtable *North American Review*.

While he was writing *Vicarious Sacrifice*, however, his familiar enemy figured as the New England theology. For Bushnell was attacking convictions New England logic had fostered for over half a century. His argument and poetry rested on the moments when moral government was broken. Sporadically but savingly in the history of the world, the retributive sequences of justice had been interrupted by love. Only these jolting intrusions upon nature's orderly penal sequences freed man for a Christian love.

143

Bushnell's protest, like his conversion, was rooted in the cultural preferences of his time. He could not use a political rationale for the faith he had seized by "the heart," and syllogisms similarly failed to appease the needs of many of his contemporaries. The sensibility that had provided a market for Mrs. Hemans and Mrs. Sigourney, for Sir Walter Scott and Lord Byron, for landscape paintings, gift books, and Jenny Lind, had for decades been giving the Taylorite cosmogony an archaic appearance. The preaching suited to Taylor's theology, Bushnell complained, produced a piety miserably lacking in "the graceful affections, . . . great sentiments, . . . inspirations." To a generation which had trembled with Mrs. Hemans, which had puzzled over and applauded Emerson, and which had read Carlyle, no further indictment was required. Describing herself as "an aspen leaf, ever trembling to the rush of some quick feeling," Mrs. Hemans portrayed the spiritual susceptibility to which gift-book poets and readers aspired. Clearly, as Bushnell announced, God had "made the world . . . for the great sentiments it will . . . bring into play."[17] By mid-century, Bushnell was ready with a theology that could meet the cravings of the romantic temper.

Possibly he had already waited too long. The realism of Howells, Twain, Lowell, De Forrest, and local colorists was gradually informing literary preferences. Popular Darwinism and business expansion were about to make the struggle for survival seem the unique expedient of progress. Yet, however gloomy the portents, Bushnell articulated a theology suited to the experiences that a more romantic era had conventionalized.

Bushnell's own interests had narrowed and intensified since the 1840's, when he first addressed himself to a generation of tender sensibilities. Now his thoughts tirelessly circled around the joined necessities of love and pain. On its higher

literary levels, American romanticism had been too concerned with individual freedom, pride, or sin to investigate
the uses of love. Yet conventions were available. In popular
novels and gift books, the dramatic power of sacrificial love
had been explored. In *Hope Leslie*, even the villain, as he
glowered over his victim, was touched by compassion. Betrayed heroines commonly died "pure, innocent, and loving," praying for their malefactors. "Father, forgive him!"
whispered the abused Maria in "The Betrayed." "He knew
not what he did." Middle-class romanticism facilitated Bushnell's concentration upon suffering love, and his exegesis
bore the marks of this pervasive literature. In one sermon,
he made the self-sacrificing love of a mother the type of
Christ's sacrifice.[18]

The gospel of the heart, the aesthetics of the responsive
sensibility, focused on the suffering Savior. "We look on him
whom we have pierced, and we are pierced ourselves."[19]
Bushnell was after a religious formulation that could re-
kindle the passion familiar to those who felt the Great
Awakening. But the agony in which redemption might be
born was not to rise from the perception of hell or God's
wrath, nor from the sinner's contrition that he had broken
the moral law; the anguish would be for the divine martyrdom that man incessantly caused.

Known guilt and redemptive sorrow attached to the image
of the crucified God. The Cross was the sole symbol that
could gather and resolve the antinomies of Christian feeling.
Nature could never express the antagonism or the union of
sin and mercy, but the Crucifixion communicated to our
"guilty feeling" the righteousness and mercy of God.

The image of divinity was reshaped to meet the requirements of the heart. God's total nature was "an immense
sensibility"; without such emotional vulnerability, He would
be unworthy of reverence. Christ necessarily suffered for

145

man's sin, for goodness itself was "nothing but a perfect feeling."[20] As God was love, He required no sacrifice to reconcile Himself to man; the atonement was not to propitiate God, but to reveal His mercy to a fearful humanity. Such a divinity could not act as a complacent watchmaker or a ubiquitous Oversoul, for the world Bushnell projected made harsh demands. Sin, suffering, disharmony, and death sustained the unremitting pain at the center of divinity.

The measure of man, as well as that of God, was taken in his emotional accessibility. Since Christ came to reconcile man to God, the efficient means of grace was the receptive sensibility. Only through the emotions could men apprehend God and achieve salvation. Regeneration required the goodness of "perfect feeling"; repentance, conversion, and sanctification hinged upon man's possibilities before the agony of Christ.

But the saving response was not easily won, for the Christ offered to faith was difficult to apprehend. A stubborn honesty informed Bushnell's reading of the New Testament, and as he perused Jesus' history, he acknowledged an odd tale, which mixed the sublime and the grotesque. The whole was a biography of "sorrow, suffering, sacrifice, death, a paradox of ignominy and grandeur not easily solved." The conclusion seemed "dark, if not weak," and the story held "severities, and repellencies and discouraging tokens." Christ cut a lonely and eccentric figure among the great men of history. "So that if we speak of heroes, we are tempted to say that he is no hero at all, or else the only hero." So dark was the story that faith depended upon the Resurrection; for unless Christ had risen, He was only a "defeated and prostrate man, covered with unutterable ignominy."[21]

Thus Bushnell again encountered the Jesus who signally failed to conform to the morality of the capitalist ethic: a stranger who concerned himself with loathsome infirmities;

who lived in passivity, meekness, and dejection; who spent his love indiscriminately on all mankind. Christ's victory was not easily known; the law of love he obeyed seemed a "law of revelation," not of intuition, and his claim to be Savior could be justified only if history were transvalued by the Resurrection.

Reviews of the *Vicarious Sacrifice* must have quickly informed Bushnell of a growing estrangement from public opinion. The laws of an atemporal redemption did not excite intellectuals, who were intrigued by the progressive march of evolution. James Freeman Clark tolerantly reminded readers of the *Christian Examiner* that they should not consider a question obsolete just because it was tedious, and he excused Bushnell's laborious, "ridiculous" effort as a necessary lesson for the foolish few who still doubted God's friendliness to man.[22]

The *North American Review* proved less clement. Bushnell's theory of Christian love was madness. Love was always proportionate to merit; to suggest that God had expended compassion upon an ignoble humanity insulted the Deity. It was an "outrage upon all love, Divine as well as human, to suppose that its subject is ever in . . . disaccord . . . with its object." Only maternal, friendly, and patriotic affections were natural and acceptable. The love of a good man for a bad man was contrary to nature, perverted, and impossible; Christ himself could not have intended the command to love one's enemies to be taken seriously.[23]

The *North American Review* thus assaulted the last outpost of Bushnell's truce with common sense. Its indictment of Christian sacrifice was lucid and total. Henceforth Bushnell would find it difficult to rest in the easy insistence on the identity between the Christian ethic and universal moral intuitions. Bushnell's antagonist aligned natural law, rational preference, and common sense against the process and obligations of a divine atonement. As he faced this new antithesis between nature and the supernatural, Bushnell needed what help he could find in America's past or present.

Contemporary allies were scarce. In Boston in 1867 and 1868 the popular spokesman for liberal orthodoxy, Mark Hopkins, lectured on "The Law of Love" and integrated self-love and benevolence in one cohesive pattern of "rational love."[24] But Bushnell did not stop with Hopkins. The scathing critique of the *North American* sent him back to Jonathan Edwards, where he found what he could scarcely have discovered in later New England thought: reinforcement for his hesitant belief that the natural and spiritual orders were discrete and alien from each other.

In 1870 Bushnell gave a sermon which was an unequivocal commitment. Invoking the distinctions of Edwards' "Nature of True Virtue," he presented the Christian Gospel as opposed to the instinctive decisions of the mind. Thus for the first time since Edwards, a major American preacher insisted on the discrepancy between the possibilities of natural, and the injunctions of Christian, love.

Following Edwards, Bushnell contrasted Christian affection with the "natural love" which was rooted in self-interest. Instinctive love issued in facsimiles of virtue: self-regard; the "sentiment of kind," which united groups and nations; and the parental love man shared with animals. Like Edwards, Bushnell denied that the love of "natural beauty" was a virtuous affection. Nor did the love of character bear the peculiar grace of virtue. "For it is the very nature of mind . . . to be attracted by goodness and beauty. . . . The worst . . . mind has sensibilities that are drawn or taken by what is lovely."

The secluded, insistent pursuit of Christian meanings had been costly. Though popular susceptibility to the categories of "the heart" had earlier lighted the course over which

Bushnell searched out the atonement's significance, the route had ended in sharp reversal. For Christian knowledge the aesthetic sensibility was useless. The love of God which paralleled the admiration of "a moral landscape" was only a kind of "lofty self-indulgence."[25] The isolation of failure, the vigilant scrutiny of Christ's sacrifice, had cut Bushnell off from the gentility of gift-book romanticism and from the easy suspirations of the "theology of the feelings." He had broken at last with the refined Calvinism which he and his colleagues had forged to meet the stringencies of social revolution.

Edwards had aided his escape, but Bushnell did not protest with the voice of Edwards only. Much as he leaned upon Edwards' distinction between natural and true virtue, the central point of his analysis was different; and of the two, Bushnell's was the more peculiarly Christian.

Edwards had measured virtue by the "consent to Being." No particular love was of value unless it derived from the "generally benevolent temper of the heart." Natural love, reaching only specific beings, had nothing to do with virtue. But true benevolence, once achieved, ascended through a series of rational preferences. A "secondary ground" of benevolence lay in the value of the object loved. Complacency, or delight in moral beauty, heightened the benevolent love that constituted true virtue, and in this "secondary ground of benevolence," proportionate to the object's worth, all true moral beauty consisted.

Bushnell did not begin with an analysis of the necessary qualities of virtue; he began with the definition of love set by Christ's sacrifice. The primary motion of Christian love was not consent but the dialectic interplay of revulsion and mercy. Christian love was a "condemning or abhorring love," without complacency in its object, "loving . . . across the gulf of displacency and disgust . . . , loving creatures

149

morally unlovely." In his ordered pattern of virtue, Edwards had provided for rational antagonisms; "if there be any Being . . . an enemy to Being in General, then . . . the truly virtuous heart" would "forsake that Being, and . . . oppose it."[26] But Bushnell insisted that divine love obliterated the hierarchies of complacency; otherwise man would never have known it.

The ecstatic union with Being, which Edwards had experienced and Emerson had recaptured, was to Bushnell won through an inexplicable, infinite mercy. Only a love that took no account of rational preference, that spent itself upon the ugly, the inimical, the repulsive, could have made an occasion fit for ecstasy in the world. Christ's life revealed the strange impetus and relentless exactions of this love and burdened man with the duty of a similar compassion.[27]

Forced to choose between a coherent, graduated love and the disordering, spontaneous passion figured in the atonement, Bushnell delineated the Christian agape. His choice was singular, sustained neither by American tradition nor by the immediate intellectual enthusiasms where future beliefs bred. Emerson's assertion that from nature the spirit could win knowledge of the eternal and his belief that all life was pervaded by upward-sweeping power were closer to the time. Where Bushnell proclaimed man's narrow escape from tragedy, bought by the death of God, Emerson chanted to the "quick cause" of efficient nature, which reached "from particles and spicular . . . to the highest symmetries, arriving at consummate results without a shock or a leap." "Nature" sang of an ascending power active through all the varied shapes of life.

> And striving to be man the worm
> Ascends through all the spires of form.[28]

Unlike Bushnell's sermon, Emerson's couplet was soon to appear prophetic. The evolutionary chain of being captured the imagination of the next generation, and its progressive sequences could not accommodate the disjunctions that for Bushnell had revealed the essential nature of God and man.

To achieve his singular perception, Bushnell had needed isolation. In 1866 a group of Unitarians and transcendentalists formed the Free Religious Association, which proposed to study Darwinism; in 1869 John Fiske accepted President Eliot's invitation to give a course of lectures at Harvard on positivism. To Bushnell the emerging intellectual climate was puzzling. For the first time since he had begun his pastorate, he spent four years without conceiving a heretical message with which to inspire and anger the world. He had no ready conceptual structure within which he could accommodate the new Darwinian science, and he wrote his postwar volumes as if Darwinism or positivism had never existed.

Two brief articles revealed that he was not oblivious of the new doctrines. But, unable to adjust them to his own perspective and reluctant to dismiss the new faith entirely, he ignored the ethic of sacrifice in his articles, just as he ignored evolution in his longer works. He was convinced that evolution jeopardized religion; yet he found it difficult to choose weapons against his latest adversaries. Darwin and Spencer construed the universe as indifferent to man and dared to ignore the instinctive human preferences that had bullied theologians throughout the century. Bushnell was ready with concessions. He would agree that the flood was local; that in the second coming the earth could not be burned, since matter was incombustible; that humanity came from many races. But how, after the strain of his own accommodations, could he accept or even understand this new philosophy and this new public, which accepted such an ignominious past and such sordid prospects without a "shock of recoil or disturbed sensibility"?

From early manhood and during the difficult years while

he worked for a hearing, Bushnell had schooled himself by the age's decree that human nature was the proper measure of the truth. Now religion was being shaken by a philosophy that defied the first laws of democratic logic and persuasion. For obviously, "if we have to choose between the eternity of Blunder and the eternity of God, it will not be difficult to settle our preferences."[29] Persistence in such odd perversity would stop the mouth of eloquence. Faintly, Bushnell may have heard the knell of the era which had been his own.

In his baffled, frenzied effort to destroy the new creed Bushnell accepted the theory of progress, urging only that an immanent God directed the process and guaranteed the world's eventual perfection. Progress had been a keynote of the age he had known and sometimes feared; it seemed to be the one commitment he now shared with alien times. Bushnell's offensive invoked the central concept of evolution, seeking only to proclaim the necessity of a God for reliable progress. Within the strategy he had chosen, Christian agape was supernumerary.

But the new order of facts and theory was eccentric to his interest. If Darwin and Spencer absorbed most intellectuals during the 1870's and 1880's, they did not hold Bushnell's attention. He was waiting for a direct personal inspiration; in 1870 revelation came. Jubilantly he wrote that he had had a communion with God more intense than ever before. The vision answered an insatiable need, for inspiration had become Bushnell's vocation. Now at last he had been granted "a new and most grand element in the conception of Christ's reconciling mission. I have had it burning in me as a most welcome fire." Once again he was justified by the promise of an original message; he had still the task of quickening theology with fresh perceptions. Insistently he described the book as "the newest thing" he had done.[30]

Yet more than ever he felt estranged, his audience unknown and undefined. He had endured four unproductive years during which he heard much of the "new radicalism." But when his vision finally came, it bypassed evolution. He was left with harassing fears. He dreaded that his solitude might have "excavated" and "undermined" his very being; he felt as "one shooting in the dark." Perhaps his long, solitary vigil had brought him only to spiritual vacancy; yet he was ardent to testify. "Where is my public?" he asked. "How shall I put this or that to be rightly taken?"[31]

The contempt of the *North American Review* had been unsettling. Though Bushnell defiantly stated the paradox of Christian love in the privacy of Hartford, *Forgiveness and the Law* stressed the identity between human and divine morality. Bushnell had been pricked by the necessity for originality, but *Forgiveness and Law* primarily repeated familiar doctrines: the reconciliation of man to God by Christ's suffering, the universal principles of obligation, the spontaneous quality of sanctification.

One new idea informed the book, reflecting Bushnell's personal struggles. Human experience, he wrote, proved the impossibility of forgiveness unless the wronged party took on himself the experiences of his malefactor. If God were to free Himself of His anger with man, He had to identify Himself with sinners. By assuming their pain, He could forgive their wrong. If Bushnell's transition from human to divine was facile, he had at last discovered an explanation of the atonement which started from God's necessities rather than man's. That in the process he had reduced God to the measure of man did not trouble him and would not trouble the generation that followed him.

Two years after publication of *Forgiveness and the Law* Bushnell died, working, characteristically, on a new aspect of Christian truth. He had been contributing a series of articles to the *Independent* on prayer, and his new manuscript, as if still answering Parker, centered on the possibility of a continual influx of the divine spirit into the receptive mind. The uncompleted, vague, and inconclusive manuscript boasted of its lack of plan. A series of thoughts on the Holy Spirit, the essay largely ignored Christ to exult in the inspirations that flowed freely from the Spirit to the human soul and brought man his highest fulfilment.

It is impossible to unite all the centrifugal messages inspiring the last decades of Bushnell's life. He had never sought consistency; now less than ever did it trouble him, though his years seemed congenial to summary and a final ordering. This extravagant indifference that scattered his thoughts reflected the discipline he had learned from his time. Seeking the comprehensive truth which included all dogmas, the formless reality which was the realm of spirit, he held the antitheses of his thought with an imperturbable flexibility. He longed to be suggestive, not definitive.

Bushnell passed the last two decades of his life in the freedom of many finalities. His career had taken fixed form; he had few driving professional fears or expectations. The pugnacity of orthodoxy had waned with time, and, despite orthodoxy, a substantial number of books testified to his originality and his fame. If he had known failure, hatred, and frustrated ambitions, he also felt that he had known God. A white beard and long white hair framed the bony, emaciated face; the eyes, remote and unappeased, dominated his sharp, prominent nose and straight, thin mouth. If his pictures do not present the face of complete success, neither do they suggest defeat, but rather an austere resignation, hardly won. "His general bearing was that of one whom life had chastened to the utmost."[32]

In the emancipation of these later years Bushnell dedicated himself to transcendent concerns. His interest was more narrowly theological than ever before. If his scrutiny of the atonement led him back to "the heart," which had been the starting point of his faith, he came to his subject transformed by the stress of persecution and partial failure. The situation, too, had changed. He could concentrate his energy upon the central doctrine of Christian belief without the distraction of widening opportunities.

His freedom issued in an understanding of the essential quality of Christianity, for which he owed little to his time and for which the time was neither ready nor eager. His perception did not bring him unstinting acclaim or a following, and consequently, it could not—even in these last years—bring him the peace of a final commitment. Yet the concept of Christian love that inspired *Vicarious Sacrifice*, and even more the 1870 sermon, stands as evidence of the unyielding search for Christianity made by a lonely, dogged, peregrine old man.

X. The Uses of Theology

In seventeenth-century New England the preacher's vocation was fixed by general consent. Called by a church of saints to teach the Gospel, he knew that the Reformed faith expounded in Calvin, Ames, and Perkins, ordered by Ramus' logic, and presented in a plain style, would re-establish the true church at the center of history. Chosen by God to reveal to the world a Holy Commonwealth, he and his people stood before men as in a "city set on a hill." Bound with his church and society in a divine covenant, he was impelled and assured by the august exigency of his shared commitment.

By 1831, when Bushnell started to prepare for the vocation he had hesitantly chosen, no such defined sphere was available to the minister. The community had expanded to a republic, which heroes of various religions had gloriously led, and the once cohesive deposit of New England faith was scattered. Within the limits of his opportunities and ability, Bushnell had to define his calling.

There was no way of finding a definitive role until he had discovered his audience and a language and procedure suited to them. As a minister, he belonged to a Taylorite Association and a General Association where Taylorites and Tylerites formed a tense, unstable union. His church was split between orthodox and liberals. And beyond Hartford were the middle classes, who believed in reform, self-improvement, and gentility, who were nervous and nostalgic about the faith of their fathers, who were affronted by Calvinistic accusations and bored by theology.

Given Bushnell's temperament, the situation was difficult. Though he was pugnacious, independent, irascible, he lacked the dogmatism and toughness necessary for prolonged combat. He hoped to include all groups in the generous comprehensiveness of his position; but as he formulated the doctrines in which he longed to unite all extremes, he found he had chiefly succeeded in becoming an enemy to be crushed or an odd, interesting stranger to be politely neglected.

Still he tried to devise a theology that could fasten the restive religious loyalties of the middle classes. In an age of oratory, his fame and influence naturally began with lectures. In 1847, on New York and Boston rostrums, he set the image of the refined East against a primitive West, and the East gave quick applause. "Such was the revelation in him of power . . . that this Boston community . . . was eager as one man for his voice, and willing to travel at his touch," Bartol wrote, recalling the impact of "Barbarism, the First Danger."[1] The 1840's were years of perturbing promise: of Unitarian blandishments, of invitations to lecture, and of the sharp isolating grace of vision.

The temper of his audience was romantic, and Bushnell's own sensibility had been shaped by the sentimental preferences of the age. Accordingly, he prized spontaneous impulses over forced control, the imagination over the reason, individual insight over formulated tradition, the heart over the head. Yet by continually checking the egotistic exuberance of romantic individualism, he held his romanticized theology within a Christian framework. *Christian Nurture* did not advocate giving free rein to the child's native impulses but insisted upon the necessary discipline of habit. If

157

God in Christ offered "God not so much to the . . . logical understanding as to the imagination and . . . esthetic apprehension of faith," the book also maintained that only traditional Christian symbols could keep man from substituting the indulgence of his ego for the experience of religion.[2]

But Bushnell did not witness a renaissance of faith conceived as the symbolic assault upon human experience. As Emerson had noted, the age was not symbolic, and by the 1850's it was evident that science, invention, and progress had captured popular imagination. Bushnell next worked to integrate geological discoveries and a new view of humanity within Christian cosmogony. *Nature and the Supernatural* described a fallen universe in which man in his freedom, power, and sin stood distinct from nature and in which God had descended to save a corrupt humanity.

The years after *Nature and the Supernatural* brought final severances. Once again Bushnell discovered he had not roused a party to a crusading faith. Now, separated from his church, he sought his vocational call in immediate revelations. He centered his thoughts on the sacrificial love of Christ. Remote at last from the shifting intellectual currents of the time, he found justification in an intimate sense of God.

Throughout most of his career, Bushnell strenuously attempted to meet the preferences of his public, but he never unbent enough for an intoxicating success. Although his American public preferred his sermons to his longer volumes, he continued to turn out theological treatises. Even the sermons of *Christ and His Salvation* exhausted the *Atlantic Monthly.* "This power of penetrating thought, so determined as . . . to wear a look of doggedness, this analysis . . . which is almost fanatical in its desire to get at the . . . reason of everything," betrayed an inconsiderate zeal. De-

158

spite the complaints of reviewers, Bushnell could not stop his probing, exacting inquiry.[3]

Bushnell in the last event carved out a peculiar role. He had not essayed a systematic moral philosophy, which customarily made textbooks rather than common reading, but neither had he been content to skitter anecdotes, paradoxes, and truisms before the public. He felt the need to impose explicit assumptions and order upon the fragmentary preferences of the time, and he set the whole within the confines of Christian theology. Because of these mixed necessities, his work stands with peculiar dignity in the history of American religious thought. He mapped the course by which orthodoxy was moving toward liberal Protestantism.. The mechanism of the movement was largely the romantic sensibility; its momentum derived from the proud experiment in democracy and the mobility of a changing economy. Bushnell's vocation and personal biography bound his fortunes with those of the middle classes, and from his sharp knowledge of his world he created works responsive enough to reflect the time's upheavals, yet searching enough to endure and reward the light of scrutiny.

Disappointed in his lifetime, Bushnell had hoped for an audience in the future. But new issues perplexed the succeeding generation, disturbed by the implications of evolution and the impact of industrialism. Bushnell's symbolism and his critique of naturalism seemed unseasonable. His exaltation of the family, however, and his faith in the Anglo-Saxon stock suited the science of later generations, and his Christ-centered theology projected for Christian reformers a vision of God which, they hoped, would move men to a wise, effective compassion.

Darwinism set the first test for sophisticated Protestant thought in the latter part of the century. By the 1880's theologians could no longer dismiss evolution as atheism, and liberal Congregationalists set about accommodating religion to the evolutionary picture of the world. Evolutionary processes seemed to provide a key to society, to history, and to the ways of God. Ministers came to Bushnell with questions and enthusiasms set by evolution, and their primary evolutionary concern delimited his possible influence. Metaphors derived from evolution shaped the religious perceptions of progressive pastors: "It is perfectly clear," Washington Gladden wrote Lyman Abbott, "that our theology must adjust itself to evolutionary conceptions; we can not now think in any other terms."[4] It proved increasingly hard to focus upon the fall of man or upon a unique redemptive event in which the eternal crossed time. By evolutionary theory, the line of development was nowhere so jagged.

Evolution brought new methods of judgment and evaluation, which obtained within the history of nature and required no transcendent illuminations. The fallen world of *Nature and the Supernatural* had disappeared; the universe itself was engaged in redemptive processes, carrying man in its beneficent upward surge. God was best manifested in the total sweep of evolution, and Christianity proved itself by winning out in the struggle for survival to be "the fittest religion."

The traditional idea of sin was revised to cohere with humanity's arduous but triumphal ascent up the chain of being. Later theologians spoke infrequently of man's rebellion against God but defined sin rather as failure to fulfil evolutionary designs. To Andover's George Harris, sin was "departure from the type," while for Lyman Abbott, Minot Savage, Henry Ward Beecher, it was a relapse into animal appetite and passion, in which man betrayed the rationality the race had so hardly won.[5]

For Bushnell, man's hope of salvation depended upon his

guilty penitence before Christ, but the new ethic seemed to require intelligent adaptation more than contrition. Savage considered evil to be the same thing as maladjustment, and George Harris promised that the good man would win in the struggle for survival, since morality was nothing but "natural selection." No transcendent God was needed to condemn poor adaptation, which evolutionary law handily penalized.[6]

The idea of regeneration was similarly reformed. To Beecher, who preached the "sin of violating the natural laws of health," regeneration was a natural stage of man's growth, while Josiah Strong and George Gordon based millennial hopes on the evolution of the brain. A speech praising Bushnell's *Christian Nurture* in 1902 pointed out that childhood training could so modify brain tissue that moral adulthood would be guaranteed.[7]

Certain of Bushnell's theories tallied with the new evolutionary emphases. In the unsettlement of these years, when many ministers felt they had to revise or give up their faith, theologians searched America's religious tradition for modes of rational belief. If the times seemed so inimical that Gladden in 1899 devoted a book to the question "What Is Left of the Old Doctrines?" he and his fellows clung to whatever seemed viable in their inherited faith and found in many of Bushnell's ideas an escape from outmoded dogma.

The men first unsettled by evolutionary theories were largely educated in America; sooner or later most of them complained that their theological education had proved inadequate. Several of such troubled, unprepared young ministers discovered a tenable faith in Bushnell. Still widely suspect as a heretic, he appealed to their own alienation from orthodoxy. "I could not have remained in the ministry an honest man," Gladden testified, "if it had not been for him. . . . If I have had any gospel to preach during the last thirty-five

years, it is because he led me into the light and joy of it."
Embattled in his small Haverhill parish, Theodore Munger
was comforted and inspired by Bushnell's successive books,
which brought new foundations for faith and confounded
orthodoxy. In Bushnell he found a deeper meaning given
the Gospel than the "arbitrary one" which prevailed.[8]

By the 1890's and 1900's Bushnell's works were listed in
the catalogues of Oberlin, Drew, the General Theological
Seminary, Yale, Bangor, Union, and Andover. Eugene Lyman testified that in the 1870's he was brought up in the
prevalent theology of Bushnell, while George Gordon found
that Bushnell's ideas pervaded Connecticut religion in the
1880's.[9]

But though Bushnell was studied, quoted, and praised, he
did not dominate later thought, which selected from his
works the ideas congenial to its prior commitments. Darwinism allowed little play for transcendent transvaluations,
and the felt disparity between God and man which had
qualified Bushnell's humanism was deplored by his admirers.
Theodore Munger regretted that his master had derogated
nature to exalt the supernatural, while John Buckham lamented that Bushnell never understood the nature evolution
had revealed. In many respects Bushnell was outmoded.
"We are not now interested," Munger explained, "except
in an antiquarian's way, in the discussion by which one
view or another of the atonement was upheld." Though
Gladden found Bushnell's essay on language a "novum or-
ganon," he had no further use for symbolic theory once
he had been freed by Bushnell's doctrine from narrow formulas. Neither he nor his contemporaries concerned themselves with structures of meaning irrelevant to scientific fact.
Science could lend no status to symbol or myth, and its
impact was too stunning for apologists to hazard unsanc-
tioned methods of belief. Criticizing Bushnell's dismissal of

"scientific theology," George Gordon announced that obviously the "unverifiable" could not form a part of "reasonable faith."[10]

Aspects of Bushnell's theology nonetheless proved persuasive to the next generations. Progressive theologians were delighted with Bushnell's insistence upon a passible Deity, bound by "the universal laws of moral obligation." The vistas of evolutionary struggle did not disturb the certainty that man was God's most reliable judge, and George Gordon and Washington Gladden centered their teaching in the moral God Bushnell had celebrated. Certain that God pervaded all stages of life, liberal theologians minimized the orthodox concept of sudden conversion and welcomed the emphasis upon slow growth in virtue, which they found in *Christian Nurture*. Sanctioned by nature, familial ties sustained man within the evolutionary totality where redemption lay. "Is not the universal and noble passion of parental love," asked Gordon, "the cord by which even the brute world is bound to the heart of God?" By the end of the century, Presbyterians and Congregationalists were testifying to the demise of the doctrine of sudden, violent conversions. Gladden was typical in his Bushnellian insistence that a "mother's holy love" could transfigure and redeem the "child's soul."[11]

The family seemed to stand as a fixed, incontrovertible value in the social and industrial upheavals of the new century. Francis Peabody expected the solution to the religious problems of the age once the family was recognized as "the type of God's Kingdom," while Walter Rauschenbusch saw in the family an institution already redeemed and incorporated the promise of *Christian Nurture* in his *Theology for the Social Gospel*.[12]

Like Bushnell, later liberal Congregationalists anticipated the reliable emergence of a Christian society from Christian homes. Munger, Abbott, and Gladden mistrusted revivals, awaiting the churchly millennium through the "law of natural increment" which Bushnell had deciphered. Liberal Protestants encouraged the spiritual hopes of the middle classes on the basis of their seemly, prosperous homes; a well-equipped house, George Harris promised, was a "perennial source of social regeneration." Gordon thought the "well-ordered, homogeneous, highly educated community" had no need of knowledge of Christ's compassion but cautioned the select few who were "Christian by inheritance" to remember that the masses required Christ.[13]

Bushnell's belief that prosperity and virtue were interlocked informed the aggressive nationalism of Josiah Strong, Austin Phelps, Lyman Abbott, and the many Protestant clergymen who supported the Spanish-American War. The metaphors of social Darwinism made Bushnell's vision of an "outpopulating Christian stock" the more persuasive. In 1899 Munger approvingly announced that events were fulfilling Bushnell's prophecy of an aggressive, virtuous, triumphant Anglo-Saxon race. Strong's *Our Country*, describing the tight-spun mesh of Christianity, prosperity, and the Anglo-Saxon race, quoted extensively from Bushnell, and Lyman Abbott enthusiastically supported the Spanish-American War, convinced that "barbarism" had "no rights which civilization is bound to respect."[14]

Inflated by middle-class assurance, evolutionary theory seemed to promise the eventual hegemony of Anglo-Saxon virtue and wealth, and in the happy expectations of militant Protestantism, Bushnell's theology proved opportune. With its doctrines of gradual development, the power of proper family training, and the hope of a dominant stock, *Christian Nurture* seemed peculiarly congenial to America's social Darwinism.

Though *Christian Nurture* fortified the class complacency

and righteous imperialism that invoked evolutionary terms, Bushnell's work served for more than the penetration of Darwinian categories into Christian thought. Protestant leaders were not content with the society that centuries of evolution had created. If the direction of advance was guaranteed, the goal was not won, and the split between Christian vision and the status quo perturbed theologians more than the logic of continual ascension should have allowed. They read Christian anticipations and values into evolution; to them Darwinism promised redemption and the Kingdom of God on earth. The Christianity they found in Bushnell and others transformed their Darwinism as decisively as Darwinism had changed their concepts of Christianity. A passion for a Christian society plagued them; distinctively Christian categories—the need of sacrifice, the Cross, salvation—gave structure to their thought.

Witnessing the tenements and crime of cities, the chicanery of trusts, the strikes and antagonism of labor, the graft of politicians, Christians were perplexed and frightened. If evolution led to the Kingdom of God, its methods so far seemed barbarous, measured by the humanized religious heritage of America. The Protestant clergy could not acquiesce in an imperfect, divided society. In their extremity ministers and laymen turned to the person of Christ for counsel. Here, too, they followed Bushnell. Though evolutionary theory implied that ideas were adjusted to successive environments, Protestant leaders looked to Jesus' teachings for the solution of contemporary problems; and though social Darwinism recommended the struggle for survival, later ministers, like Bushnell, found the law of Christian experience in sacrifice.

Evolution revealed warfare, pain, and defeat in the process of the universe, and it seemed susceptible of a Christian reading only if God Himself endured the suffering and

165

victimization that pervaded time. Bushnell's picture of a God marked by sorrow and anguish from the beginning of the world met the necessity; and Savage, Smyth, and Harris commented on the prevalence of his atonement theory. Gladden, George Gordon, and William Adams Brown saw in Christ the expression of the essential compassion of God, who suffered eternally because of His perfect love. "The God of the stellar universe," Rauschenbusch testified, "is a God in whom I drown." Only the "modified Sabellianism" of Bushnell offered him a God he could understand and love, a God who had "always suffered with and for mankind."[15]

Liberal theologians took up Bushnell's ideas with the greater alacrity because they had neither the public nor the time to worry through theological complexities. Without caviling over theory, they rapidly moved to practical questions. What they wanted from Christianity was not the personal assurance of salvation but the impetus to a new society, not release from God's wrath but the creation of effective human compassion. Christ's love set the example which human love could follow. The atonement served to galvanize man's energetic pity and initiate a new society. To Rauschenbusch, the Crucifixion stood as the primary incentive to the sacrificial love leading toward the Kingdom; it was "the most tremendous publicity success in the history of mankind."[16]

But if later theologians repeated Bushnell's doctrine of Christian sacrifice, the love they enjoined marched with nature, not against it. Moved by the descent of God, Bushnell had preached the strangeness of the Christian imperative of love; the next generation, anxious to establish the coherence between evolutionary progress and triumphant Christianity, rejected any such breach with nature. At Andover, Harris announced the harmony between the laws of Christianity and evolution, stressing that self-love was Christian and sacrificial love an aspect of group survival. Relieved to find that evolution involved protection of the young and herd loyalties, theologians identified these natural relationships with the Christian law of sacrificial love. Christ, explained William Clarke, had set forth "a law of natural love." The "virile, authoritative, rational" love of progressive theology had little in common with the passionate martyrdom Bushnell had deciphered in the Cross.[17]

Eventually Jesus as teacher eclipsed Bushnell's vision of a crucified and saving God. Buckham regretted that Bushnell had placed Jesus on the divine side of the "chasm" he had foolishly opened between God and man. Bushnell's Christology had focused on the atonement, but later theologians disparaged the shadowy Christ of Pauline faith in favor of the persuasive reality of the historic Jesus. Arguing that the symbolism of the Cross had no place in modern life, Edward Ames suggested that a more timely Christianity would stress Jesus' hostility to the Pharisaic law, his scourging of the money-changers, his blessing of children.[18]

The first requirement the new theology made of Christ was that he indicate the way to the good society. If Jesus had failed to solve the "temperance problem," Abbott was nonetheless inspired at the thought of the "superb prison warden" He would have made, and the pastor saw Christ's mission as the attempt to elevate the masses to wealth and wisdom. Bushnell had primarily demanded a converting change in the quality of the emotional life; for him the extraordinary love created by knowledge of Christ served to express a saving faith, not to reorder the world. But later theologians derogated the emotional religion of the past. Bushnell had warned that a society concealing sin by its manifest reforms was evil and delusive, but Rauschenbusch exulted that "a Christian social order makes bad men do good things." Liberal Christians hastened to disengage the

instructive "teachings" of Jesus from a cumbersome theology, and in the unsettlement of rapid social change laymen
and ministers in chautauqua courses, Sunday schools, and
discussion groups sought the reassurance of moral stability
which knowledge of Jesus' ideas might bring.[19]

The churchmen who followed Bushnell had their own
peculiar problems to meet. Like Bushnell, they were addressing the middle-class public rather than scholars or theologians. Because of their public and because they were more
anxious to comprehend modern science and society through
Christian concepts than to preserve a theological tradition,
they borrowed and discarded with easy hands. They were
dedicated not to conserving the whole of theology but to
saving Christianity from anachronism.

From Bushnell's work they derived courage, inspiration,
and renewed faith. His rationale served as a point of departure in their campaign to defend essential Christianity. The
qualified naturalism of *Christian Nurture*, the humanized
Deity of *God in Christ*, and the human freedom and power
described in *Nature and the Supernatural*, answering their
needs, became constant motifs in liberal Protestantism.
That their Darwinism awaited a Kingdom of God on earth,
won through sacrifice and love, must be partly attributed to
Bushnell. Bushnell's theology proved useful in the battle of
the next half-century for a humane, enlightened, viable
Christianity. Inevitably, in the exigencies of the times, many
of his ideas were neglected. Yet, in their generous flexibility
and their energetic dedication, Bushnell's successors continued his tireless, loyal quest for a living Christian faith.

Notes

INTRODUCTION

1. William W. Sweet, *The Story of Religion in America* (New York, 1939), pp. 322–24; William Sprague, *Annals of the American Pulpit* (New York, 1857), Vol. I.

CHAPTER I

1. Mary Bushnell Cheney, *Life and Letters of Horace Bushnell* (New York, 1880), pp. 3–24.

2. Horace Bushnell, *Christian Nurture* (New York, 1860), p. 333.

3. Cheney, *op. cit.*, p. 29.

4. *Ibid.*, p. 32; Henry Beers, *Nathaniel Parker Willis* (Boston, 1885), pp. 51, 43–44.

5. Jonathan Brace, Jr., letter to his father, 1827 (Brace Papers, Yale University Library); Cheney, *op. cit.*, pp. 36, 40–46.

6. Cheney, *op. cit.*, pp. 36, 40.

7. *Ibid.*, p. 208.

8. Dwight, *Summer Tours; or, Notes of a Traveller* (2d ed.; New York, 1847), pp. 512–20.

9. Eliza Leslie, "The Quilting," *The Pearl* (Philadelphia, 1833), pp. 93–116; Catherine Sedgwick, "The Fashionable Boarding School," *The Pearl* (Philadelphia, 1833), pp. 17–43; Ann Stephens, "The Blind Pastor," *The Religious Souvenir* (New York, 1840), pp. 241–49; S. C. Edgarton, "The Rustic Wife," *Rose of Sharon* (Boston, 1841), pp. 137–65.

10. Sarah Hale, *Studies of American Character* (Boston, 1829), pp. 49–80; P. H. E., "Fire by Night," *The Religious Souvenir* (New York, 1840), pp. 254–62; Stephens, *op. cit.*

169

11. "The First Shade of Thought," *Rose of Sharon* (Boston, 1840), p. 235; E. A. Bacon, "The Knitting Society," *Rose of Sharon* (Boston, 1842), p. 78; Isabel Drysdale, "A Church in the Backwoods," *Christian Offering* (Boston, 1832), p. 10.

12. *The Young Lady's Own Book: A Manual of Intellectual Improvement and Development* (Philadelphia, 1832), p. 14.

13. Edward Lawrence, *Life of the Reverend Joel Hawes* (Boston, 1881), p. 70.

14. Odell Shepard, *Pedlar's Progress: The Life of Bronson Alcott* (Boston, 1937), pp. 41, 60–63; Ray Palmer, *An Address on the Ministry of the Future* (Albany, 1857), pp. 7–10; Enoch Pond, *Young Pastor's Guide* (Bangor, 1844), pp. 19–20; Gardiner Spring, *The Power of the Pulpit* (New York, 1848), p. 373.

15. Cheney, *op. cit.*, pp. 47–48.

16. Bushnell, "Remarks to His Students on Leaving Yale College" (MS address, Yale Memorabilia Collection, Yale University Library), pp. 2–7.

17. Bushnell, *Work and Play* (New York, 1864), pp. 396–400.

18. Cheney, *op. cit.*, p. 59.

19. *Ibid.*, p. 56.

CHAPTER II

1. Mary Bushnell Cheney, *Life and Letters of Horace Bushnell* (New York, 1880), p. 59.

2. W. S. Dutton, "Notes on Taylor on Mental Philosophy" (MS in Yale University Library), p. 41 and *passim*.

3. Captain Thomas Hamilton, *Men and Manners in America* (Edinburgh, 1833), I, 131–32; Alexis de Tocqueville, *Democracy in America* (New York, 1945), II, 3–8.

4. *Op. cit.*, p. 11.

5. J. P. Thompson, "Orthodox Unitarians," *New Englander*, V (1847), 579.

6. Lyman Beecher, *Autobiography*, ed. Charles Beecher (New York, 1866), II, 230.

7. E. F. Burr, "Christianity a Strong System," *New Englander*, XVII (1859), 847.

8. Ebenezer Porter, *Lectures on Homiletics and Preaching* (New York, 1844), p. 131; "Professor Park's Memoir of Dr. Emmons," *New Englander*, XIX (1861), 714.

9. Timothy Dwight, *Theology; Explained and Defended in a Series of Sermons* (Middletown, Conn., 1819), III, 478.

10. Albert Barnes, "How Can the Sinner Be Made To Feel His Guilt?" *Christian Spectator*, V (1833), 172.

11. Ralph W. Emerson, *Complete Works*, ed. E. W. Emerson (Boston, 1876–83), X, 329.

CHAPTER III

1. Ralph W. Emerson, *Journals* (Boston, 1909–14), VI, 266; "Coleridge," *Princeton Review*, XX (1848), 144–86. See also Lemuel Grosvenor, "Coleridge's View of the Atonement," *Biblical Repository*, XII (1844), 177–88; Henry Neill, "Thoughts on the Atonement," *Biblical Repository*, V³ (1849), 381–414.

2. Samuel T. Coleridge, *Aids to Reflection* (London: Bohn Library, 1913), p. 66.

3. Dr. A. M. Goodwin, "Dr. Bushnell's *Sermons for the New Life*," *New Englander*, XVII (1859), 39; J. M. Hoppin, "Bushnell's *Sermons on Living Subjects*," *New Englander*, XXXI (1873), 98.

4. Coleridge, *op. cit.*, pp. 148, 168.

5. *Ibid.*, p. 136; Mary Bushnell Cheney, *Life and Letters of Horace Bushnell* (New York, 1880), p. 209.

6. Coleridge, *op. cit.*, p. 197.

7. *Ibid.*, p. 235.

8. Marsh, "Preliminary Essay," in Coleridge, *op. cit.*, pp. xxxi–xliv; Shedd, *Homiletics and Pastoral Theology* (New York, 1873), pp. 413–14.

9. Cheney, *op. cit.*, pp. 86–88, 144–49, 276–77; Bushnell, *Work and Play* (New York, 1864), pp. 455 ff.; Bushnell, Journals (MSS in Yale Divinity School Library), Vols. I–IV; Bushnell, *Building Eras in Religion* (New York, 1881), p. 233.

10. See Irving Babbitt, *Rousseau and Romanticism* (Boston, 1919).

11. Bushnell, "On Moral Agency" (MS in Sterling Library).

12. Cheney, *op. cit.*, p. 68.

CHAPTER IV

1. Samuel Goodrich, *Recollections of a Lifetime* (New York, 1857), I, 436.

2. Mary Bushnell Cheney, *Life and Letters of Horace Bushnell* (New York, 1880), p. 67.

3. Mary K. Talcott, "Prominent Business Men," in James

Trumbull (ed.), *Memorial History of Hartford County, Connecticut, 1663–1884* (Boston, 1887), I, 665; Henry Erving, *The Connecticut River Banking Company* (Hartford, 1925); J. Eugene Smith, *One Hundred Years of Hartford's "Courant"* (New Haven, 1949), pp. 170, 174, 239, 321.

4. Smith, *op. cit.*, p. 239.

5. Lydia H. Sigourney, *Letters of Life* (New York, 1866), p. 293; Talcott, *op. cit.*, p. 665; Henry Gall and William Jordan, *One Hundred Years of Fire Insurance* (Hartford, 1919), p. 43.

6. Smith, *op. cit.*, p. 242; Charles Burpee, *A Century in Hartford* (Hartford, 1931), chaps. i–iii; Patrick Woodward, *One Hundred Years of the Hartford Bank* (Hartford, 1892), pp. 145–46.

7. Henry Baldwin, "Social Life after the Revolution," in Trumbull (ed.), *op. cit.*, I, 588–603; Sigourney, *op. cit.*, p. 282.

8. Edward Lawrence, *Life of the Reverend Joel Hawes* (Boston, 1881), pp. 53, 99.

9. Baldwin, *op. cit.*, p. 603.

10. Gordon Haight, *Mrs. Sigourney: The Sweet Singer of Hartford* (New Haven, 1930), pp. 17–35; Henry Beers, "Hartford in Literature," in Trumbull (ed.), *op. cit.*, I, 164–68.

11. Charles G. Finney, *Memoirs* (New York, 1876), p. 419; Lawrence, *op. cit.*, pp. 54–55.

12. *New England Religious Herald* (Hartford), January 24, 1846; Smith, *op. cit.*, p. 251.

13. Smith, *op. cit.*, pp. 162, 248–49; *Report of the Executive Committee Young Men's Institute* (Hartford, 1846).

14. Smith, *op. cit.*, pp. 58–59.

15. Henry Barnard, *Tribute to Gallaudet* (Hartford, 1852), p. 20.

16. Hawes, *Memoir of Normand Smith; or, the Christian Serving God in His Business* (American Tract Society, 1839), p. 3.

17. Bushnell, *Sermons on Living Subjects* (New York, 1872), pp. 264–65, 267.

18. Barnard, *op. cit.*, pp. 16–20, 63, 83–90.

19. Bushnell, *Moral Uses of Dark Things* (New York, 1868), p. 226.

20. Charles G. Finney, *Lectures on Systematic Theology* (Oberlin, 1878), p. 156; see also "The Influence of Christianity upon Public Morals," *Christian Review*, VIII (1837), 495; "Christian Obligation with Respect to the Conversion of the World," *Biblical Repository*, II (1832), 320.

21. "Mercantile Morals and the Successful Merchant," *Princeton Review*, XXV (1853), 230.

22. Bushnell, *Sermons on Living Subjects*, pp. 248, 263.

23. Hawes, *op. cit.*, pp. 23–26.

24. Thomas Weaver, *A Historical Sketch of the Police Service of Hartford* (Hartford, 1900), p. 37; John C. Noonan, *Nativism in Connecticut, 1829–1860* (Washington, 1938), pp. 83, 233; Thomas McManus, "Roman Catholic Church," in Trumbull (ed.), *op. cit.*, I, 26–27; Smith, *op. cit.*, p. 233; Odell Shepard, *Pedlar's Progress: The Life of Bronson Alcott* (Boston, 1937), p. 272.

25. Smith, *op. cit.*, pp. 244–46.

26. *Ibid.*

27. Bushnell, *Building Eras in Religion* (New York, 1881), p. 82.

28. George Stewart, Jr., *A History of Religious Education in Connecticut to the Middle of the Nineteenth Century* (New Haven, 1924), pp. 289–90, 298.

29. Bushnell, *Sermons for the New Life* (New York, 1858), p. 330.

30. Stewart, *op. cit.*, pp. 297, 338.

31. *Ibid.*, p. 297.

32. Smith, *op. cit.*, pp. 253, 227.

33. Bushnell, *Work and Play* (New York, 1864), p. 63; *A Discourse on the Slavery Question* (Hartford, 1839), pp. 11–13.

34. Bushnell, *Moral Uses of Dark Things*, p. 303.

35. Letter from Bushnell to Leonard Bacon, April 18, 1843 (Yale Memorabilia Collection, Yale University Library).

36. Lawrence, *op. cit.*, pp. 55–57, 64.

37. Sigourney, *op. cit.*, p. 283; "Unitarian and Episcopalian Affinities," *New Englander*, III (1845), 557–59.

38. *Diary of Thomas Robbins, D.D.*, ed. Increase Tarbo (Boston, 1887), II, 213.

39. Gordon W. Russell, "Important Votes and Comments," in *Contributions to the History of Christ Church* (Hartford, 1895), I, 246, 340, and *passim*.

40. *Ibid.*, p. 300.

41. George Walker, *History of the First Church in Hartford* (Hartford, 1884), pp. 370–80; Baldwin, *op. cit.*, p. 588.

42. Hawes, *A Sermon Delivered at the Dedication of the North Congregational Church of Hartford* (Hartford, 1825), pp. 15–16.

43. Carlos Wilcox, *Remains, with a Memoir of His Life* (Hartford, 1828), pp. 65 ff.

44. William Sprague, *Annals of the American Pulpit* (New York, 1857–60), II, 657.

45. North Church *Records* (State Historical Society, Hartford), Vol. I.

46. "On Preaching," *Christian Spectator*, II (1825), 642; Samuel Miller, *The Difficulties and Temptations Which Attend Preaching of the Gospel in Great Cities* (Baltimore, 1820).

47. May E. Gambrell, *Ministerial Training in Eighteenth Century New England* (New York, 1937), p. 106.

48. Bushnell, Journals (MSS in Yale Divinity School Library), Vols. I, V.

49. Bushnell, *A Discourse on the Slavery Question*, p. 117; *Views of Christian Nurture* (2d ed.; Hartford, 1848), p. 177.

50. Bushnell, *Building Eras in Religion*, pp. 19, 152; *Spirit in Man* (New York, 1903), pp. 106–7, 118; *Christ and His Salvation* (New York, 1864), p. 276.

51. *Spirit in Man*, pp. 137, 144.

52. *Ibid.*, pp. 117, 139–42.

53. *Sermons on Living Subjects*, p. 289; *Society and Religion: A Sermon for California* (San Francisco, 1856), p. 22; *Spirit in Man*, pp. 126–29.

54. *Sermons on Living Subjects*, p. 248; *Society and Religion*, p. 22.

55. *Sermons for the New Life*, pp. 108, 206–9, 315; *Christ and His Salvation*, p. 74; "The Word 'Grace' Revived" (MS sermon in Yale Divinity School Library); "On Communion" (MS sermon in Yale Divinity School Library); *Sermons on Living Subjects*, pp. 53, 112; *Spirit in Man*, p. 45.

56. *Spirit in Man*, pp. 118–20, 281; *Sermons on Living Subjects*, pp. 334, 378 ff.

57. "The Church Catalogue of Rome" (MS sermon in Yale Divinity School Library); "Power from on High" (MS sermon in Yale Divinity School Library).

58. *Sermons for the New Life*, pp. 330–45.

59. Bushnell, "American Politics," *The American National Preacher*, XIV (New York, 1840), 199; *Women's Suffrage: The Reform against Nature* (New York, 1869), pp. 9 ff.

60. *Christ and His Salvation*, pp. 130–31; *Moral Uses of Dark Things*, pp. 314–15.

61. *Moral Uses of Dark Things*, pp. 174–75.

CHAPTER V

1. Bushnell, *Views of Christian Nurture* (2d ed.; Hartford, 1848), p. 247.

2. Timothy Tuttle, "A Permanent Ministry," *Contributions to the Ecclesiastical History of Connecticut* (New Haven, 1861), pp. 239–40; Francis Wayland, *Letters on the Ministry of the Gospel* (Boston, 1863), pp. 124–25; Thomas Skinner, *Aids to Preaching and Hearing* (New York, 1839), p. 70; William G. T. Shedd, *Homiletics and Pastoral Theology* (New York, 1873), pp. 245–46; Nehemiah Adams, "On a Certain Success in Pulpit Eloquence," *Bibliotheca Sacra*, II (1845), 702.

3. *Views of Christian Nurture, loc. cit.*

4. Enoch Pond, *The Young Pastor's Guide* (Bangor, 1844), p. 138; Charles Finney, *Lectures on Revivals of Religion* (Oberlin, 1868), pp. 175–76.

5. Bushnell, "Duty Not Measured by Our Own Ability" (MS sermon in Yale Divinity School Library); "Sermon on Hosea 6:3" (MS sermon in Yale Divinity School Library); Mary Bushnell Cheney, *Life and Letters of Horace Bushnell* (New York, 1880), p. 7.

6. Letter from Bushnell to President Day, Hartford, February 16, 1836; *Views of Christian Nurture*, pp. 3–4.

7. Bushnell, "Parting Words" (MS sermon in Yale Memorabilia Collection, Yale University Library), p. 16.

8. Letter from George Gale to Charles Finney, quoted in Arthur Cole, *Social Ideas of the Northern Evangelists* (New York, 1954), p. 80; North Church *Records* (State Historical Library, Hartford), Vol. I; L. Eaton, "Eli Todd," *New England Quarterly*, XXVI (1953), 435–53.

9. Gardiner Spring, *Power of the Pulpit* (New York, 1848), p. 631; "Reverend Finney's *Lectures on Revivals of Religion*," *Religious Magazine*, III (1836), 103.

10. Thomas Brownell, *Errors of the Times* (Hartford, 1843).

11. Graham Taylor, "The Fourth Congregational Church," in James Trumbull (ed.), *Memorial History of Hartford County, Connecticut, 1663–1884* (Boston, 1887), pp. 392–93.

12. Sarah Pomeroy, "Whittier's Residence in Connecticut," *Connecticut Magazine*, XI (1907), 571.

13. Henry Barnard, *Tribute to Gallaudet* (Hartford, 1852), p. 271; Finney, *Memoirs* (New York, 1876), p. 419.

14. John Abbott, *The Mother at Home* (New York, 1833), p.

NOTES TO PAGES 58-62

15; Alexander, "The Merchant's Clerk Cheered and Counselled," in William Sprague (ed.), *The Man of Business Considered in His Various Relations* (Philadelphia, n.d.), p. 35; "Large Cities," *Christian Spectator*, I² (1828), 21.

15. *Congregational Visitor*, I (1844), 71.

16. James Matthew, *The Religious Influence of Mothers* (New York, 1836), p. 310; Abbott, *op. cit.*, pp. 148-49; Gardiner Spring, *Hints to Parents* (New York, 1833), p. 10; Catherine Sedgwick, *Home* (Boston, 1839), p. 54; Lydia H. Sigourney, *Letters to Mothers* (Hartford, 1838), pp. 14-17; A. B. Muzzey, *The Fireside* (Boston, 1854), p. 6.

17. William Howell, "Shrines," *Friendship Offering* (1841), and "Childhood," *Rose of Sharon* (1841), p. 118.

18. *Christian Nurture* (New York, 1860), p. 373.

19. Abbott, *op. cit.*, p. 154; Channing, *Works* (Boston, 1868), III, 289; "An Address to Christians on Family Religion," *Christian Disciple*, I (1813), 11; "Richard and His Mother," *Congregational Visitor*, II (1845), 106-7; "Nursery Maxims," *Religious Magazine*, III (1836), 87.

20. Frank L. Mott, *Golden Multitudes* (New York, 1947), pp. 306-7; Anne L. Kuhn, *The Mother's Role in Childhood Education* (New Haven, 1947), pp. 43 ff.; Mott, *A History of American Magazines, 1741-1860* (New York, 1930), p. 487.

21. George Stewart, *A History of Religious Education in Connecticut to the Middle of the Nineteenth Century* (New Haven, 1924), p. 169; Carlos Wilcox, *Remains, with a Memoir of His Life* (Hartford, 1828), pp. 168 ff.; Lewis Schenck, *The Presbyterian Doctrine of Children in the Covenant* (New Haven, 1940), pp. 82 ff.

22. Edward Lawrence, *Life of the Reverend Joel Hawes* (Boston, 1881), p. 26.

23. William Sprague, *Annals of the American Pulpit* (New York, 1857-60), Vol. I, *passim*.

24. Peter DeJong, *The Covenant Idea in New England Theology* (Grand Rapids, Mich., 1945), pp. 175 ff.; Joseph Bellamy, *Works* (New York, 1811-12), II, 455-509; W. S. Dutton, "Notes on Taylor's Lectures in Mental Philosophy" (MS in Yale University Library); Nathanael Emmons, *Works*, ed. Jacob Ide (Boston, 1860), III, 590-635.

25. *Seventeenth Annual Report of the American Sunday School Union* (Philadelphia, 1841), p. 36; *Eighteenth Annual Report . . .*

176

(Philadelphia, 1842), p. 14; John Todd, *The Sabbath School Teacher* (Northampton, 1856), p. 86.

26. John Nevin, *The Anxious Bench* (2d ed.; Chambersburg, Pa., 1844), pp. 64, 124, 130–36.

27. Edwin Rice, *The Sunday School Movement* (Philadelphia, 1917), p. 141; *Twelfth Annual Report of the American Sunday School Union* (Philadelphia, 1836), pp. 13–14; *Twenty-fifth Annual Report* . . . (Philadelphia, 1849), p. 21.

28. *Letters of Pestalozzi on the Education of Infancy* (Boston, 1830), pp. 44–49; Todd, *op. cit.*, p. 88; Abbott, *op. cit.*, pp. 145–46.

29. Abbott, *op. cit.*, pp. 102–13; Muzzey, *op. cit.*, p. 174; Sedgwick, *op. cit.*, p. 54.

30. Nevin, *op. cit.*, pp. 124–36.

31. Hodge, *Essays and Reviews* (New York, 1857), p. 310; Schenck, *op. cit.*, pp. 84 ff.

32. North Church *Records*, I, 95 ff.; *Christian Nurture* (1860), p. 61; Cheney, *op. cit.*, p. 92; Curtis Geer, *The Hartford Theological Seminary, 1834–1934* (Hartford, 1934), p. 46.

33. Bushnell, review of *Errors of the Times*, in *New Englander*, II (1844), 166–67; "The Kingdom of Heaven as a Grain of Mustard Seed," *ibid.*, II (1844), 600–19.

34. Bushnell, Journals (MSS in Yale Divinity School Library), Vol. V.

35. *Christian Nurture* (1860), p. 28 and *passim*.

36. *Ibid.*, pp. 227–49, 317–18.

37. *Ibid.*, p. 10.

38. *Ibid.*, pp. 289–93.

39. *Views of Christian Nurture* (2d ed., 1848), pp. 61, 173–74.

40. Ralph W. Emerson, *Journals* (Boston, 1909–14), II, 94; *ibid.*, V, 298; *Views of Christian Nurture* (2d ed., 1848), p. 228.

41. Alexander, *Thoughts on Preaching* (New York, 1869), p. 42; "On Sitting in Public Prayers," *Christian Observatory*, II (1848), 297; John Dix, *Pulpit Portraits* (Boston, 1854), pp. 39–40; review of *Christian Nurture*, in *Christian Observatory*, I (1847), 418; T. F. C., "The Baptist and Pedobaptist Theories of Church Membership," *Christian Review*, XII (1847), 547.

42. Bennet Tyler, *Letters to Dr. Bushnell on Christian Nurture* (Hartford, 1848), pp. 6 ff.

43. G. W. Briggs, "Bushnell on Christian Nurture," *Christian Examiner*, XLIII (1847), 448; Noah Porter, Jr., "Bushnell on Christian Nurture," *New Englander*, VI (1848), 126–34.

44. Bushnell, "On Moral Agency" (MS in Yale University Library); *Sermons for the New Life* (New York, 1858), pp. 54, 64.

45. *Christ and His Salvation* (New York, 1864), pp. 368–70.

CHAPTER VI

1. Gannett, "The Relation of the Pulpit to Future Ages: A Defence of Preaching," *Christian Examiner*, XLIV (1848), 437.

2. "The Pulpit," *Christian Spectator*, I (1824), 634–35; "The Pulpit," *Religious Magazine*, II (1835), 203; "Difficulties in Parishes," *Christian Examiner*, IX (1830), 9; James Alexander, *Thoughts on Preaching* (New York, 1869), p. 42.

3. See William Sprague, *Annals of the American Pulpit* (New York, 1857–60), Vol. I, *passim;* Ralph W. Emerson, *Journals* (Boston, 1909–14), II, 448; Orville Dewey, *Autobiography and Letters* (Boston, 1883), p. 370; Edwards Park, "Duties of a Theologian," *Biblical Repository*, II² (1839), 374–75; "The Impressiveness of Teaching," *New Englander*, V (1847), 98; Henry J. Ripley, *Sacred Rhetoric* (Boston, 1849), p. 133.

4. Mary Bushnell Cheney, *Life and Letters of Horace Bushnell* (New York, 1880), p. 68; John Weiss, *Life and Correspondence of Theodore Parker* (New York, 1864), I, 103; Dewey, *op. cit.*, p. 39.

5. See Edward Parker, *The Golden Age of American Oratory* (Boston, 1857).

6. Ralph W. Emerson, *Complete Works*, ed. E. W. Emerson (Boston, 1876–83), VII, 65–66.

7. Edwards Park, *The Duties of the New England Clergy* (Andover, 1844), p. 36; George Shepard, "Manner in the Preacher," *Biblical Repository*, IV² (1843), 81; "On the Proper Length of Religious Services," *Christian Spectator*, IV (1822), 634; Emerson, *Journals*, V, 280–81.

8. "On Calling Young Men to the Ministry," *Christian Observatory*, II (July, 1848), 349.

9. "Reviews," *Christian Spectator*, I³ (1829), 236; Alexander, *op. cit.*, p. 40.

10. Alexander, *op. cit.*, p. 47; Theodore Bacon, *Leonard Bacon: A Statesman in the Church* (New Haven, 1931), p. 150; Arthur C. McGiffert, *Young Emerson Speaks* (New York, 1938), p. 76; "Literary Notices," *New Englander*, II (1844), 486.

11. Arthur Cole, *Social Ideas of the Northern Evangelists*

NOTES TO PAGES 77–85

(New York, 1954), p. 220; Gardiner Spring, *Power of the Pulpit* (New York, 1848), p. 446.

12. Cheney, *op. cit.*, p. 90.

13. Letter from Bushnell to Leonard Bacon, January 1, 1835 (Yale University Library); Alexis de Tocqueville, *Democracy in America* (New York, 1945), I, 306; Bushnell, *American Politics* (New York, 1840), p. 151; *Crisis of the Church* (Hartford, 1835), p. 36.

14. See Cole, *op. cit.*, pp. 144 ff.

15. Bushnell, *Politics under the Law of God* (Hartford, 1844), p. 200 and *passim*.

16. Bushnell, *Moral Uses of Dark Things* (New York, 1868), p. 66.

17. *Politics under the Law of God*, pp. 6 ff.

18. Bushnell, *The Northern Iron* (Hartford, 1854), p. 10; Bushnell, *The Census and Slavery* (Hartford, 1860), p. 4.

19. *Politics under the Law of God*, Preface.

20. Cheney, *op. cit.*, p 91, 96–97, 104.

21. Bushnell, *A Discourse on the Slavery Question* (Hartford, 1839), p. 21.

22. Letter from Bushnell to Leonard Bacon, Hartford, April 18, 1843 (Yale University Library).

23. Bushnell, "The Evangelical Alliance," *New Englander*, V (1847), 113, 121–23.

24. Rev. H. Tappan, "Romanism and Barbarism," *Biblical Repository*, IV[3] (1848), 252–82.

25. Cheney, *op. cit.*, pp. 191–92.

26. *Ibid.*, p. 2.

27. G. W. Briggs, "Bushnell on Christian Nurture," *Christian Examiner*, XLIII (1847), 435; "Bushnell's *God in Christ*," *Biblical Repository*, V[3] (1849), 371; "The Law of Human Progress," *Princeton Review*, XVIII (1846), 2; Payne Kilbourne, *A Biographical History of Litchfield County, Connecticut* (New York, 1851), p. 355.

28. Cheney, *op. cit.*, p. 90.

29. Enoch Pond, *Review of Dr. Bushnell's "God in Christ"* (Bangor, 1849), p. 104.

30. Bushnell, Journals (MSS in Yale Divinity School Library), Vol. III; Frank B. Carpenter, "Studio Talks with Dr. Bushnell," *Independent*, LII (January 11, 1900), 117–18.

31. Emerson, quoted in F. O. Matthiessen, *American Renaissance* (New York, 1941), p. 22.

32. "Thoughts on the State of Theological Science and Education in Our Country," *Bibliotheca Sacra*, I (1844), 736.

33. Emerson, *Journals*, VIII, 205.

34. William Russell, *Pulpit Elocution* (2d ed.; Andover, 1869), pp. 79 ff.

35. Ripley, *op. cit.*, p. 194; "The Preaching for the Age," *New Englander*, XII (1854), 11; Samuel Brown, "The Studies of an Orator," *Biblical Repository*, V^2 (1841), 270–72; Cheney, *op. cit.*, p. 210.

36. "The Impressiveness of Teaching," *New Englander*, V (1847), 91; W. S. Buddington, "Robertson's Sermons," *New Englander*, XVII (1859), 866–70; Calvin Pease, "The Distinctive Idea of Preaching," *Bibliotheca Sacra*, X (1853), 388; George Shepard, "The Effective Preacher," *Biblical Repository*, I^2 (1839), 355.

37. Parker, *op. cit.*, pp. 340–41, 353; Bushnell, *Building Eras in Religion* (New York, 1881), pp. 182–84.

38. Bushnell, *Sermons for the New Life* (New York, 1858), pp. 27–41; *Building Eras in Religion*, pp. 188, 196.

39. Constance Rourke, *Trumpets of Jubilee* (New York, 1927), p. 178; Edwards Park, Introduction, in Russell, *op. cit.*, p. 17; David Mears, *Life of Edward Norris Kirk* (Boston, 1877), p. 327; Bushnell, "Revelation" (MS sermon in Harvard University Library).

40. Noah Porter, Jr., "Coleridge and His American Disciples," *New Englander*, IV (1847), 165; Park, "Duties of a Theologian," *op. cit.*, p. 370.

41. Orville Dewey, *Discourses on Various Subjects* (2d ed.; New York, 1835), p. 165; Park, *The Duties of the New England Clergy*, p. 47.

42. "Wordsworth and His Poetry," *Christian Spectator*, VIII^3 (1838), 133; W. H. Goodrich, "The Preaching for the Age," *New Englander*, XII (1854), 12; James Flint, "Brazier's Sermons," *Christian Examiner*, XLVI (1849), 436; Joseph Thompson, "Unitarianism in New York," *New Englander*, V (1847), 22.

43. "The Religious Influence of Taste," *Christian Spectator*, I (1824), 363; Charles White, "The Conservative Element in Christianity," *Bibliotheca Sacra*, IX (1852), 541–42; Park, "The Proper Mode of Exhibiting the Truth," *Biblical Repository*, X^1 (1838),

472–73; Edwin Holt, "Review of Park's Life and Writings of the Reverend William Bradford Homer," *Biblical Repository*, VIII² (1842), 191; Park, "The Theology of the Intellect and of the Feelings," *Bibliotheca Sacra*, VII (1850), 545; Brown, *op. cit.*, p. 272.

44. Preface, *The Christian Keepsake for 1838*, p. vii; Park, "The Theology of the Intellect and of the Feelings," *op. cit.*; "American Poetry," *Christian Review*, II (1837), 192; S. C. Edgarton, Preface, *Rose of Sharon* (Boston, 1841), p. 5.

45. Bushnell, *Work and Play* (New York, 1864), p. 265; "Taste and Fashion," *New Englander*, I (1843), 153–58.

46. Park, "The Proper Mode of Exhibiting Theological Truth," *Biblical Repository*, X¹ (1838), 446; Brown, *op. cit.*, p. 270; *Work and Play*, p. 34.

47. Park, "Theology of the Intellect and of the Feelings," *op. cit.*, pp. 536–61.

48. Cheney, *op. cit.*, p. 213; Bushnell, *God in Christ* (Hartford, 1849), p. 92.

49. Bushnell, "Revelation"; *Work and Play*, p. 34.

CHAPTER VII

1. Mary Bushnell Cheney, *Life and Letters of Horace Bushnell* (New York, 1880), p. 200.

2. *Ibid.*, p. 90.

3. Bayley Fox, *Hints to Sunday School Teachers* (Boston, 1840), p. 126.

4. Stuart, "Scriptural Views on Imputation," *Biblical Repository*, VII (1836), 325–26; "Moses Stuart," *New Englander*, X (1852), 47–52.

5. "Moses Stuart."

6. Channing, *Works* (Boston, 1868), III, 95.

7. *Ibid.*, pp. 11, 75, 177, 196; IV, 140.

8. Dewey, *Discourses and Reviews* (New York, 1847), pp. 63, 118; Andrews Norton, *Tracts concerning Christianity* (Cambridge, Mass., 1852), pp. 63–65.

9. Edward Hitchcock, *Religion of Geology* (Boston, 1851), p. 6.

10. W. S. Dutton, "Notes on Taylor's Lectures in Mental Philosophy" (MS in Yale University Library).

11. John Locke, *Essay on the Human Understanding* (London,

1690), Book III, chap. i, sec. 5; Dugald Stewart, *Elements of the Philosophy of the Human Mind* (Philadelphia, 1793), p. 10.

12. Hugh Blair, *Lectures on Rhetoric and Belles Lettres* (Pittsburgh, 1829), p. 67; Stewart, *op. cit.*, pp. 160–64.

13. Blair, *op. cit.*, pp. 134, 159; Stewart, *op. cit.*, p. 164; Timothy Dwight, *Theology; Explained and Defended in a Series of Sermons* (Middletown, 1819), IV, 306; Henry Kames, *Elements of Criticism* (4th ed.; London, 1769), I, 83–94.

14. Reed, *Observations on the Growth of the Mind* (Boston, 1826), p. 46; "On the Power of Moral Painting in Sermons," *Quarterly Christian Spectator*, N.S., II (1828), 458; Bushnell, "Revelation" (MS sermon in Harvard University Library).

15. Johnson, *A Treatise on Language, or, the Relation Which Words Bear to Things* (New York, 1836), pp. 17, 20, 251, and *passim*.

16. Emerson, *Complete Works*, ed. E. W. Emerson (Boston, 1876–83), I, 30–32; Porter, *Lectures on Homiletics and Preaching* (New York, 1844), p. 147; Gibbs, *Philological Studies with English Illustrations* (New Haven, 1857), p. 15.

17. Francis Hubbard, "Study of the Works of Nature," *Biblical Repository*, VI (1835), 173–81; Bushnell, "Revelation."

18. Bushnell, *God in Christ* (Hartford, 1849), pp. 30, 38, 102.

19. Bushnell, *Spirit in Man* (New York, 1903), p. 358; *God in Christ*, p. 78.

20. Heinrich Brunner, *Die Mystik und das Wort* (2d ed.; Tübingen, 1928), chap. i.

21. Wilhelm Dilthey, *Leben Schleiermachers* (Berlin, 1870), I, 444.

22. Emerson, *Journals* (Boston, 1909–12), X, 235; *Works*, I, 45; *Journals*, VI, 273–74.

23. *God in Christ*, pp. 77, 82.

24. Channing, *op. cit.*, III, 146.

25. *God in Christ*, pp. 74, 111.

26. Cheney, *op. cit.*, p. 298.

27. *God in Christ*, pp. 176, 265–66; *Building Eras in Religion* (New York, 1881), p. 281.

28. *God in Christ*, pp. 69, 73, 90; *Building Eras in Religion*, pp. 252–72.

29. *Building Eras in Religion*, pp. 252, 272; *God in Christ*, p. 38.

30. Emerson, *Journals*, VI, 18; *Poetry and Prose of Walt Whitman*, ed. Louis Untermeyer (New York, 1949), p. 114; Bushnell,

"The Word 'Grace' Revived" (MS sermon in Yale Divinity School Library).

31. Emerson, *Works*, XI, 18–21; Bushnell, "The Lord's Supper" (MS sermon in Yale Divinity School Library).

32. *God in Christ*, pp. 103–4, 254; Emerson, *Journals*, VI, 189.

33. *God in Christ*, pp. 189, 204, 302.

34. *Ibid.*, p. 308.

35. "Unitarian and Episcopalian Affinities," *New Englander*, III (1845), 361.

36. J. H. M., "Bushnell's Discourses," *Christian Examiner*, XLVI (1849), 463, 475–76.

37. Cheney, *op. cit.*, p. 219.

38. Review of *God in Christ*, in *Biblical Repository*, V³ (1849), 371 ff.; review of the Reverend Robert Turnbull's *Theophany*, *ibid.*, p. 564; Enoch Pond, *Review of Dr. Bushnell's "God in Christ"* (Bangor, 1849), p. 113; Charles Hodge, *Essays and Reviews* (Bangor, 1849), p. 113.

39. Pond, *op. cit.*, p. 115; "Recent Doctrinal and Ecclesiastical Conflicts in Connecticut," *Princeton Review*, XXV (1853), 634; Frank Carpenter, "Studio Talks with Dr. Horace Bushnell," *Independent*, LII (1900), 120; Orestes Brownson, *Works* (Detroit, 1884), VII, 1; Edwards Park, *Discourses* (Andover, 1885), p. 105; review of *God in Christ*, in *Biblical Repository*, V³ (1849), 559; Cheney, *op. cit.*, pp. 245–46.

40. Cheney, *op. cit.*, pp. 234–46.

41. *Ibid.*, p. 222; Bushnell, untitled MS sermon in Yale Divinity School Library.

42. Cheney, *op. cit.*, p. 248.

43. *Ibid.*, p. 451.

CHAPTER VIII

1. Mary Bushnell Cheney, *Life and Letters of Horace Bushnell* (New York, 1880), pp. 251, 265, 267, 322–24, 352.

2. *Ibid.*, p. 375.

3. *Ibid.*, p. 326.

4. *Ibid.*, pp. 304, 451.

5. *Ibid.*, p. 362.

6. *Ibid.*, pp. 322, 361, 391.

7. *Ibid.*, p. 277.

8. Bushnell, *Work and Play* (New York, 1864), pp. 100–101;

Nature and the Supernatural (New York, 1858), pp. 17–28, 134, 453, 511, 515, 521; *Sermons for the New Life* (New York, 1858), p. 427.

9. *Nature and the Supernatural*, p. 470.

10. Cyrus Bartol, "Dr. Furness and Dr. Bushnell: A Question of Words and Names," *Christian Examiner*, LXVI (1859), 121.

11. *Nature and the Supernatural*, p. 19.

12. Moses Stuart, "A Critical Examination of Some Passages in Genesis 1:7," *Biblical Repository*, VII (1836), 55.

13. Edward Hitchcock, *The Religion of Geology* (Boston, 1851), pp. 5–8; James Dana, "Science and the Bible," *Bibliotheca Sacra*, XIII (1856), 91.

14. George Fisher, *Life of Benjamin Silliman* (New York, 1866), I, 355–60, 364–80; Hitchcock, *op. cit.*, Preface; review of Agassiz's *Natural History*, in *Atlantic Monthly*, I (1858), 322.

15. John J. Dana, "Claims of Science on the Ministry," *Bibliotheca Sacra*, VI (1849), 464; "The Mosaic Cosmogony," *New Englander*, IX (1851), 75.

16. Hitchcock, *Religious Truth, Illustrated from Science* (Boston, 1857), p. 70; James Dana, *op. cit.*, p. 109; *ibid.*, XIV (1857), 399; "Religion of Geology," *Bibliotheca Sacra*, XVII (1860), 697; "Short Notices," *Princeton Review*, XXIII (1851), 165.

17. Silliman, Appendix, in Robert Bakewell, *An Introduction to Geology* (New Haven, 1829), pp. 6–7; James Dana, *op. cit.*, XIV (1857), 399; E. P. Barrows, "The Mosaic Narrative of the Creation," *Bibliotheca Sacra*, XIII (1856), 373; James Dana, *op. cit.*, XIV (1857), 512; *ibid.*, XIII (1856), 631–32; John Means, "The Narrative of the Creation in Genesis," *Bibliotheca Sacra*, XII (1855), 106; Ralph Waldo Emerson, *Complete Works*, ed. E. W. Emerson (Boston, 1876–83), III, 179–80.

18. *Nature and the Supernatural*, p. iii.

19. Stephen Whicher, *Freedom and Fate: An Inner Life of Ralph Waldo Emerson* (Philadelphia, 1953), p. 142; O. B. Frothingham, "Man and Nature in Their Religious Relations," *Christian Examiner*, LIV (1853), 461, 463, 464; W. H. Furness, "Nature and Christianity," *Christian Examiner*, XLIII (1847), 42–46.

20. *Nature and the Supernatural*, pp. 76–78, 208–10.

21. Arthur Ekirch, Jr., *The Idea of Progress in America, 1815–1860* (New York, 1944), pp. 102, 124.

22. *Ibid.*, p. 128; Bushnell, *Building Eras in Religion* (New York, 1881), p. 52.

23. Frothingham, *op. cit.*, p. 468; *Nature and the Supernatural*, p. 420.

24. Noah Porter, Jr., "Theodore Parker," *New Englander*, II (1844), 374 ff.; see Perry Miller (ed.), *The Transcendentalists* (Cambridge, Mass., 1952), chap. v.

25. Porter, *op. cit.*, p. 360.

26. Cheney, *op. cit.*, pp. 310–11; *Nature and the Supernatural*, p. 525.

27. *Nature and the Supernatural*, p. 513.

28. *Ibid.*, pp. 240, 518; *Work and Play*, pp. 3–43.

29. Emerson, *op. cit.*, I, 65; *Nature and the Supernatural*, p. 193.

30. *Nature and the Supernatural*, p. 171.

31. *Ibid.*, p. 101.

32. *Ibid.*, p. 232.

33. *Ibid.*, p. 276.

34. Hopkins, *Evidences of Christianity* (Boston, 1871), p. 228; Furness, *op. cit.*, p. 35.

35. *Sermons for the New Life*, pp. 94, 103.

36. Cheney, *op. cit.*, pp. 419–20.

37. Bartol, *op. cit.*, pp. 115, 118, 121.

38. Cheney, *op. cit.*, pp. 420, 422.

CHAPTER IX

1. H. M. Goodwin, "Dr. Bushnell's *Sermons for the New Life*," *New Englander*, XVII (1858), 382, 388–89.

2. Mary Bushnell Cheney, *Life and Letters of Horace Bushnell* (New York, 1880), pp. 422, 445; Bushnell, *Nature and the Supernatural* (New York, 1858), p. 527; Bushnell, *Forgiveness and the Law* (New York, 1874), p. 92.

3. Cheney, *op. cit.*, pp. 448–49.

4. *Ibid.*, p. 533.

5. *Ibid.*, p. 449.

6. *Ibid.*, p. 540; Theodore Munger, *Horace Bushnell, Preacher and Theologian* (New York, 1899), p. 116.

7. *Building Eras in Religion* (New York, 1881), p. 311.

8. *Ibid.*, p. 318.

9. Cheney, *op. cit.*, p. 479.

10. *Ibid.*, pp. 541–42.

11. *Ibid.*, pp. 435, 445–46.

12. Nathanael Emmons, *Works*, ed. Jacob Ide (Boston, 1860), pp. 24–44.

13. Ralph Waldo Emerson, *Complete Works*, ed. E. W. Emerson (Boston, 1876–83), II, 271, 296.

14. Bushnell, *Christ and His Salvation* (New York, 1864), p. 267.

15. Bushnell, "God Reigns for the Largest Love" (MS sermon in Yale Divinity School Library).

16. *Vicarious Sacrifice* (New York, 1866), p. 47.

17. *Ibid.*, p. 526; Lydia H. Sigourney, "Introductory Essay," *Works of Mrs. Hemans* (Philadelphia, 1840), I, xxxi; *Christ and His Salvation*, p. 265.

18. Mrs. Perkins, "The Bitter Cup," *Rose of Sharon* (Boston, 1855), p. 207; T. Shepard, "The Betrayed," *Christian Souvenir* (1840), p. 40; Catherine Sedgwick, *Hope Leslie* (New York, 1827), II, 36.

19. *Vicarious Sacrifice*, p. 154.

20. *Christ and His Salvation*, pp. 244, 261–62.

21. *Vicarious Sacrifice*, pp. 177, 197, 215, 216, 218.

22. James F. Clark, "Bushnell on the Vicarious Sacrifice," *Christian Examiner*, LXXX (1866), 360 ff.

23. Review of *Vicarious Sacrifice*, in *North American Review*, CII (1866), 557–64, 571.

24. Mark Hopkins, *The Law of Love, and Love as a Law* (New Haven, 1869), p. 55.

25. "God Reigns for the Largest Love."

26. *Ibid.*; Jonathan Edwards, "The Nature of True Virtue," in *Jonathan Edwards*, ed. Clarence Faust and Thomas Johnson ("American Writers Series" [New York, 1935]), p. 356.

27. See Perry Miller, "Edwards to Emerson," *New England Quarterly*, XII (1940), 589–623. Anders Nygren (*Agape and Eros*, trans. A. G. Herbert [London, 1932]) makes the distinction between Christian and pagan concepts of love upon which I draw in these pages (see esp. pp. 52–56, 118–40).

28. Emerson, *op. cit.*, III, 179; II, 1.

29. Bushnell, "Science and Religion," *Putnams' Magazine*, I (1868), 269; "Progress," *Hours at Home*, pp. 201, 204, 206, and *passim*.

30. Cheney, *op. cit.*, pp. 517–18, 526–27.

31. *Ibid.*, pp. 523–24, 525, 539.

32. *Ibid.*, p. 534.

CHAPTER X

1. Mary Bushnell Cheney, *Life and Letters of Horace Bushnell* (New York, 1880), p. 185.
2. *God in Christ* (Hartford, 1849), p. 102.
3. Review of *Christ and His Salvation*, in *Atlantic Monthly*, XV (1865), 377.
4. Quoted in Ira Brown, *Lyman Abbott, Christian Evolutionist* (Cambridge, Mass., 1953), p. 147.
5. Harris, *Moral Evolution* (Boston, 1896), pp. 418, 424; Abbott, *Theology of an Evolutionist* (Boston, 1899), pp. 109-10; Beecher, *Evolution and Religion* (New York, 1885), pp. 75 ff.; Savage, *Religion of an Evolutionist* (Boston, 1876), pp. 99-105.
6. Savage, *op. cit.*, p. 100; Harris, *op. cit.*, p. 418.
7. James Parton, "Henry Ward Beecher's Church," *Atlantic Monthly*, XXIX (1867), 44; Beecher, *op. cit.*, p. 98; Strong, *Our Country* (New York, 1886), p. 169; Gordon, *The Christ of Today* (Boston, 1886), pp. 300-301; William Mutch, "Bushnell and Christian Nurture," *Bushnell Centenary* (Hartford, 1902), pp. 119-20.
8. Quoted in Munger, *Horace Bushnell, Preacher and Theologian* (Boston, 1899), p. 375; Washington Gladden, *Recollections* (Boston, 1909), pp. 119-20; Benjamin Bacon, *Theodore Thornton Munger, New England Minister* (New Haven, 1913), p. 49.
9. Gordon, *My Education and Religion* (New York, 1925), p. 214; Lyman, "Christian Thought and a Spiritualistic Philosophy," in Vergilius Ferm (ed.), *Contemporary American Theologians* (New York, 1925), II, 105.
10. Buckham, *Progressive Religious Thought in America* (Boston, 1919), p. 24; Gladden, *op. cit.*, p. 119; Bacon, *op. cit.*, pp. 384-86.
11. Gordon, *The Christ of Today*, p. 89; Gladden, *What Is Left of the Old Doctrines?* (Boston, 1899), p. 238; Robert Thompson, *History of the Presbyterian Church* ("American Church History Series," Vol. VI [New York, 1895]), p. 239; William Horton, "Rough Sketch of a Half-formed Mind," in Ferm (ed.), *op. cit.*, I, 181.
12. Peabody, *Jesus Christ and Christian Character* (New York, 1903), p. 287; Rauschenbusch, *Theology for the Social Gospel* (New York, 1917), p. 226.
13. Bacon, *op. cit.*, p. 45; Abbott, *Reminiscences*, pp. 465-66; Gladden, *The Christian Pastor and the Working Church* (New

York, 1898), p. 387; Harris, *op. cit.*, p. 358; Gordon, *The Christ of Today*, pp. 274–77.

14. Strong, *op. cit.*, Introduction; Munger, *op. cit.*, p. 84; Brown, *op. cit.*, pp. 173 ff.

15. Gladden, *What Is Left of the Old Doctrines?* pp. 166–75; Harris, *op. cit.*, p. 489; Newman Smyth, *Progressive Orthodoxy* (Boston, 1886), pp. xxvii, 230–32; Gordon, *The Christ of Today*, p. 179; William Brown, *How To Think of Christ* (New York, 1945), p. 283; Rauschenbusch, *op. cit.*, p. 179; Doris Sharpe, *Walter Rauschenbusch* (New York, 1942), p. 322.

16. Rauschenbusch, *op. cit.*, p. 269.

17. Harris, *op. cit.*, p. 422; Clarke, *The Idea of Jesus* (New York, 1911), p. 120; Peabody, *op. cit.*, p. 122.

18. Buckham, *op. cit.*, p. 28; Ames, "Theory in Practice," in Ferm, *op. cit.*, II, 19.

19. Abbott, *Jesus of Nazareth: His Life and Teachings* (New York, 1869), p. 111, and *Christianity and Social Problems* (Boston, 1896), p. 318; Charles Hopkins, *The Rise of the Social Gospel in American Protestantism* (New York, 1940), chap. xii.

A Bibliographical Comment

The following summary notes only the books that proved particularly helpful in preparation of this study. My doctoral dissertation, from which the present work was adapted, contains a complete bibliography and can be found in Widener Library, Cambridge, Massachusetts.

The Spirit in Man, edited by Mary Bushnell Cheney (New York, 1903), contains selections from the important sermons that Bushnell left unpublished. The complete manuscript of the crucial sermon "God Reigns for the Largest Love" adds valuable material, however. The five handwritten Journals of the trip to Europe, though largely dutiful records of the dimensions of churches visited, are interesting as the only record in diary form which Bushnell kept. Mary Bushnell Cheney's *Life and Letters of Horace Bushnell* (New York, 1880), presents his correspondence, writings, and personal life from a daughter's point of view.

For understanding of the religious tradition in which Bushnell worked, Perry Miller's *The New England Mind* (New York, 1939) and *Jonathan Edwards* (New York, 1949) are essential. Frank H. Foster's *A Genetic History of New England Theology* (Chicago, 1907) is lucid, though rather narrowly focused on the question of free will. Joseph Haroutinian's *Piety vs. Moralism: The Passing of New England Theology* (New York, 1932) traces the complex theological changes that subtly transformed the Calvinism of the Puritans into a rationalistic moralism. Two works by European scholars made it possible to set Bushnell's contributions to theology in broader perspective. Heinrich Brunner's *Die Mystik und das Wort* (2d ed.; Tübingen, 1928) discriminates between Christian faith and Schleiermacher's mysticism, and Anders Nygren's *Agape and Eros*, translated by A. G. Herbert

(London, 1932), brilliantly defines the disparity between Pauline *agape* and pagan *eros*.

Contemporary ideas affecting Bushnell's thought include the theories of Unitarians and transcendentalists, the restatements of orthodoxy, and the new beliefs resulting from science. Perry Miller's *The Transcendentalists* (Cambridge, Mass., 1950) presents and interprets the contending issues and theories centered around transcendentalism. Charles Feidelson's *Symbolism and American Literature* (Chicago, 1953) is a suggestive, occasionally orphic analysis of the semantic and symbolic theories of mid-century American writers. The writings of Edwards Park present the modifications of orthodoxy made by an Andover professor in response to pressures similar to those Bushnell experienced in his Hartford pulpit, while the essays of Alexander Hodge reveal the difficult, indignant course of an intransigent orthodoxy. The impact of science on American middle-class thought has been comprehensively analyzed in Arthur Ekirch's *The Idea of Progress in America, 1815–1860* (New York, 1944).

Autobiographies and biographies suggest how Bushnell's fellow ministers met the intellectual and professional challenge of the times. William Sprague's *Annals of the American Pulpit* (8 vols.; New York, 1857–60) is an exhaustive picture of the eighteenth- and nineteenth-century ministry, drawn from letters by contemporaries. The autobiographies of Lyman Beecher and Charles Finney convey the robust, unintellectualized evangelism of the churches, while Orville Dewey's *Autobiography and Letters* (Boston, 1883) reveals the attitudes of a successful Unitarian minister. Sidney Mead's *Nathaniel W. Taylor, 1786–1858* (Chicago, 1942) incisively portrays the interplay between American republican society and Taylor's New Divinity. Constance Rourke's *Trumpets of Jubilee* (New York, 1927) offers a dramatic, vivid picture of several ministers. The only biography of the dominant, dogmatic, and learned Alexander Hodge is the outdated *Life* by A. A. Hodge (New York, 1880).

Many of the interests and worries of the society Bushnell addressed are reflected in the best-selling gift-book literature. The widely sold *Mother at Home* by John Abbott (New York, 1833) anticipates many of the doctrines of *Christian Nurture*. The *Annual Reports* of the American Sunday School Union reveal some of the theological strains the Sunday school attempted to ease. Articles in religious periodicals like the *Christian Examiner*

(Unitarian), the *Princeton Review* (Presbyterian), and the *Biblical Repository* and *Bibliotheca Sacra* (Congregational) present the dilemmas of the ministry as they were immediately experienced. Some of the tensions between Christian faith and mercantile society are documented in Joel Hawes's *Memoir of Normand Smith; or the Christian Serving God in His Business* (American Tract Society, 1839). The basic interpretation of the links between Protestant thought and capitalism is, of course, Max Weber's *The Protestant Ethic and the Spirit of Capitalism*, translated by Talcott Parsons (New York, 1930). The particular society Bushnell encountered in Hartford had to be pieced out of many sources. J. Eugene Smith's *One Hundred Years of Hartford's "Courant"* (New Haven, 1949) provided the most detailed and comprehensive picture of the city.

Bushnell's influence on later theology is brought out in the many tributes progressive Christians wrote to him: T. T. Munger's *Horace Bushnell, Preacher and Theologian* (Boston, 1899), John W. Buckham's essay in *Progressive Religious Thought in America* (Boston, 1919), Washington Gladden's remarks in his *Recollections* (Boston, 1909). The integration of the humanitarian Christianity inherited from Bushnell and others with evolution is attempted in Lyman Abbott's *The Theology of an Evolutionist* (Boston, 1897) and Minot Savage's *The Religion of an Evolutionist* (Boston, 1876). The most intricate and ambitious synthesis of the ethics of love and survival is George Harris' *Moral Evolution* (Boston, 1899). The ideology of the social gospel is thoroughly summed up in Charles Hopkins' *The Rise of the Social Gospel in American Protestantism, 1865–1915* (New Haven, 1940). Walter Rauschenbusch's *A Theology for the Social Gospel* (New York, 1917) is the only serious contemporary effort to articulate the theology behind social Christianity.

Index

Abbott, John, *Mother at Home*, 63
Abbott, Lyman, 137, 160, 164, 167
Adam, 127
Aetna Fire Insurance Company, 33, 34
African Free Church, Hartford, Connecticut, 38
Agape; *see* Love
Agassiz, Louis, 123
Alcott, Bronson, 8
Alexander, James, 58, 70, 76
American Sunday School Union, 62
Ames, Edward, 167
Ames, William, 156
Amherst College, 97, 122
Andover Theological Seminary, 8, 21, 26, 87, 88, 89, 90, 91, 94, 95, 99, 100, 123, 160, 162, 166
Anglo-Saxons, 57, 71, 124, 159, 164
Anti-Christ, 50
Apollinarianism, 111
Apthorp, Mary, 29
Aristotle, 125
Arminianism, 41
Atlantic Monthly, 121, 158
Atonement: moral-government theory of, xi, xii, 139; in New England theology, xii, 139; Bushnell on, 134, 137, 139, 142, 143, 146, 149, 153, 155, 166, 167; James F. Clarke on, 148; in liberal Protestantism, 162, 166

Bacon, Leonard, 81, 83, 111
Baptism, 64, 65, 66
Baptists, xiii
Barnum's museum, 88

Bartol, Cyrus, 84, 93, 111, 116, 117, 126, 132, 157
Beecher, Henry Ward, 35, 87, 88, 91, 92, 134, 160, 161
Beecher, Lyman, 18, 29, 30, 54, 77, 81, 83, 140; *Plea for the West*, 82
Bellamy, Joseph, 17, 44, 62, 109
Benton, Thomas Hart, 35
Bible: and Bushnell, 21, 117, 119, 123; and Bushnell's congregation, 47; and language, 95, 96; and science, 97, 120, 121, 122, 125; Bartol on, 132
Biblical Repository, 75, 82, 83, 87, 88, 89, 90, 95, 100, 111
Bibliotheca Sacra, 95, 121, 122
Blair, Hugh, 14, 98
Blake, William, 71
Boston, Massachusetts, 38, 82, 84, 90, 93, 94, 104, 113, 114, 116, 121, 148, 157
Boston and Springfield Railroad, 32
Brace, Jonathan, Jr., 4
Brace, Thomas, 34
Brown, Thomas, 14
Brown, William Adams, 166
Brownell, Bishop Thomas, 35, 56, 66, 76; "Errors of the Times," 56, 57
Brownson, Orestes, 111
Buckham, John, 162
Bunyan, John, *Holy War*, 115
Bushnell, Horace
  Biography: childhood, 1–3; relations with parents, 3–4; conversion, 3, 11, 20, 137, 144; college, 4–6, 10, 12; conflicts